Your Worthiness Cycle

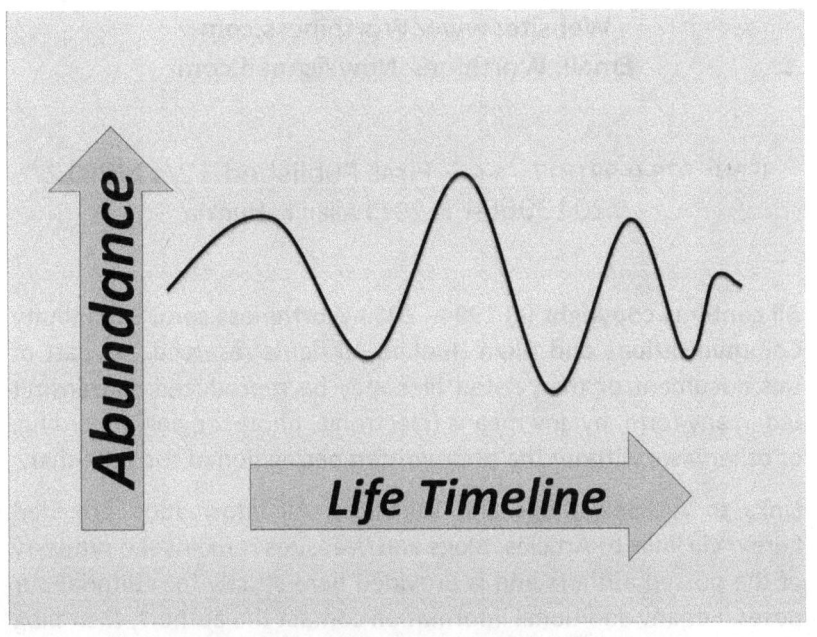

*A Breakthrough Method to
Unleash Your Power to Manifest
The Life You've Always Wanted*

By

Allan K. Hunkin

Author of *"Finding Better Solutions Faster"*

Publisher Information

Published by Worthiness.com and Equanimity Communications

For Editorial & Bulk Order contact

Worthiness.com: 252 - 8623 Granville Street
Vancouver Canada - V6P5A2

Website: www.Worthiness.com
Email: WorthinessNow@gmail.com

ISBN: 978-0-9918171-4-6 – First Published 12/12/2012
V20130604 © 2013 Allan K. Hunkin

All contents copyright (c) 1994 - 2013 Worthiness.com. Equanimity Communications and Allan Hunkin. All rights reserved. No part of this document or the related files may be reproduced or transmitted in any form, by any means (electronic, photocopying, recording, or otherwise) without the prior written permission of the publisher.

Links to Articles, Blogs and Websites: All information provided herein via links to Articles, Blogs and Websites remains the property of the posted authors and is provided here strictly for editorial purposes. For any additional information contact the authors, their blog or the website on which the piece was posted.

Limit of Liability and Disclaimer of Warranty: The publishing company has used its best efforts in preparing this book, and the information provided herein is provided "as is." Worthiness.com and/or Allan Hunkin make no representation or warranties with respect to the accuracy or completeness of the contents of this book, and specifically disclaims any implied warranties of merchantability or fitness for any particular purpose and shall in no event be liable for any loss of profit or any other commercial damage, including but not limited to special, incidental, consequential, or other damages.

Trademarks: This book identifies product names and services known to be trademarks, registered trademarks, or service marks of their respective holders. They are used throughout this book in an editorial fashion only. In addition, terms suspected of being trademarks, registered trademarks, or service marks have been appropriately capitalized, although Worthiness.com and Allan Hunkin cannot attest to the accuracy of this information.

Use of a term in this book should not be regarded as affecting the validity of any trademark, or service mark. Worthiness.com and/or Allan Hunkin is not associated with any product or vendor mentioned in this book.

Declaration of integrity: If you have this file (or a printout) and didn't pay for it, you are depriving the author and publisher of their rightful royalties. Please purchasing a copy at Worthiness.com All order information and news is kept current at Worthiness.com. A portion of your declaration of integrity will be donated to a Charity chosen by the publisher.

Other books by Allan Hunkin:

>*Finding Better Solutions Faster*
>*Where Do I Go From Here?*
>*From Fire to Light*

Listen to '*Creating Elegant Solutions*' with Allan Hunkin at:

http://www.spreaker.com/user/allanhunkin

Join us on: Facebook -.facebook.com/WorthinessNow

Twitter - twitter.com/WorthinessNow

YouTube - youtube.com/user/allanhunkin

LinkedIn – linkedin.com/in/allanhunkin

For more information visit: www.Worthiness.com

To book Allan for radio and speaking engagements contact Maureen Collins (worthinessnow@gmail.com)

Early praise for 'Your Worthiness Cycle'

"Allan has combined his extensive business experiences, creativity, research, and training to develop a totally new personal growth technology. The day I took his seminar I felt we'd changed the world."

~ Shivan Skipper, Radical Clarity Photography

In his down to earth, conversational style, liberally sprinkled with humorous, touching personal anecdotes and detailed charts and diagrams, Allan illustrates the inexplicable hidden patterns that govern our lives, and shows us ways to gain mastery over them. Bravo!

~ Shelora Fitzgerald, Certified Hand Analyst and Life Coach

"Allan creates an atmosphere for self discovery. He presents ideas for healing and backs them up with his own personal experiences. His passion for personal growth is infectious and his content is invaluable."

~ Pauline Stevenson, Woman in Management Program

Allan K. Hunkin is "a lamplighter for our Time"

~ John Bradshaw, Author 'The Homecoming'

"Worthiness isn't something that a person thinks about very often, (I suspect rarely, if my experience is the norm), especially as you define the term in your book. Your approach to life change coaching is quite unique, and it gave me pause for thought often as you carefully guided me through the thought processes as you outlined them. The reader can't help but find new direction in their life as they progress through the book.

~ Samantha Perrin, Life Coach and Certified PSYCH-K© Facilitator

Dedication

Many years ago a dear friend by the name of Dennis and I were sitting around, watching the world go by. It was a beautiful day and we were soaking up the warm sun. It was peaceful but I was troubled. "Dennis," I said, "I am in real trouble with my son. He just won't listen to me. I want the best for him but he seems to hate all the self-help audios I play for his benefit when we're out driving. I want him to be really successful and I know if he learns this stuff when he's young he'll get a real head start on what he needs to know to go all the way to the top."

"But right now," I added, "I don't think he'd throw water on me if I was on fire. The more I try to help him the more he runs away. I'm supposed to be a hot shot in Personal Development for heaven's sakes . if I can't even help my own son then who am I really?"

Dennis, who had more love and wisdom in his little finger than I have in my whole body, continued soaking in the peaceful day and said nothing. I was about to ask him if he'd dozed off when he said:

> "I think you are giving him answers to questions
> he hasn't even thought up yet."

In a millisecond I knew that I would remember those words for the rest of my life. I found it so profound that I was speechless (which if you know anything about me is rare). With all the great self-help literature I had read and the world-famous thought leaders I call friends, without a shadow of a doubt I had never read or heard anything so wise. I promised myself that I would keep it fresh in my mind to pull out when I encountered someone who was doing what I was with my son.

Everyone one of us needs the answers to some key questions... who am I?, Why am I here?, Does God exist?, What is the meaning of all this anyway? At some point you gain the awareness that everyone will have to ask those questions, but hopefully you have also learned that you get to choose which questions, when you want ask them, in what order, and of whom. *To give others the answers first is to rob them of the distance they need to travel in order to know what to ask and why.*

In the movie 'The Natural' Roy Hobbs (played by Robert Redford), is visited in hospital by Iris Gaines (Glenn Close), a woman with whom he had a brief encounter many years before. She bore a son but never told Roy. Filled with regrets about his career and a woman who had killed herself in front of him, he talks about what he had planned and how his life actually turned out. Iris brings a profound truth, for all of us, to his life review:

> "I believe that we have two lives: the one we learn with, and the one we live with after that."

This book is about gaining fresh insight into new levels of awareness which have the power to fundamentally head your life in a new and exciting direction. My wonderful friend Dennis was the catalyst for the creation of this book.

Dennis has since passed but much of the fresh insights, wisdom and heart he drops into my mind every day is contained within the pages of this book.

"Dennis... thank you so much old friend... I owe you a beer big time and I can't wait to see you as soon as I'm done here."

My Sincere Appreciation

I would like to thank the following friends, family and associates for Expertise, Advise and Encouragement given so generously:

Shelora Fitzgerald Shelora.com who advised, debated and argued with me every step of the way. This book is much better for it.

David Rawlings Trupanion.com has been a mentor and advisor on this project and many others I have been involved in.

Samantha Perrin (SamanthaPerrin.ca) Samantha took it upon herself to edit the second version which I thought was mistake free. It wasn't.

Gina Leigh added a level of encouragement as well an edit of the final draft of the book.

In the first incarnation of this book Olga Sheean (OlgaSheean.com) supported this work with ideas, encouragement. She hosted the first seminar on Worthiness in her living room. Photographer Shivan Skipper (500px.com/Shivan) did all the original graphics for *'The Worthiness Cycle.'* Janice Laing provided continual guidance.

Kerry Gullins, (gullinsconsulting.ca), Nichole Dermody, Judy Yates, Georgie (Toronto), Maxine (Las Vegas), Michael and Masenn Jonsin (Scottsdale) thank you all so much for all that you contributed.

Thanks also to Michael and Masenn Jonsin who provided safe haven and made it possible for me to get back on track.

Introduction

"Worthiness is a state us within where our resistance we have accumulated to Success, Happiness and Fulfillment is no longer in control."

Hello... Allan Hunkin here. Let me ask you a question...

Are you worthy?

Are you worthy of having all of the things you've dreamed of having?

Yes, of course you are worthy. You are worthy of every good thing that life has to offer.

There is *'no such thing'* as an 'un-worthy' person. Unworthiness actually does not exist.

But . . . a lack of awareness and understanding of what worthiness REALLY is and how it works is costing you every day in attracting and receiving the things you want out of life.

Worthiness is NOT a state like self esteem or self worth. There is no switch you can turn on where you are suddenly worthy. There is no Worthiness gene or upper level of IQ where some people are endowed with the ability to soak up all of life's riches.

Worthiness is not static. Worthiness is a **'cycle'** and operates as a wave. Like a wave, it rises and falls according to a number of factors in your life, both past and present. Some of these factors you can point to, such as having a stormy childhood. Some you understand, but most of the important factors are hidden in your subconscious and unconscious mind. Many worthiness factors are invisible yet they are a determining factor in what you think is possible for you and how long it takes for you to reach your goals.

Knowing where you are at any given moment in your personal worthiness cycle will help mitigate the ups and downs of life and help you lift yourself higher each time you are on the upside of the cycle. Recognizing certain recurring themes, patterns and indicators of your cycle will help you to not drop as low as you have before on the down side of your cycle. The higher you go in the cycle, and the longer you stay 'up,' the more of life's riches are available to you.

Understanding your Worthiness Cycle, and how to use it to create the life you want, is one of the most important things you will ever learn about yourself. It is also one of the most important things you will learn about others because it gives you a much deeper understanding of why people do the things they do. Understanding others' motivations and tendencies puts you out ahead of people, situations and events, providing you with opportunities you likely would not have recognized before.

The minute you learn Worthiness principles you will no longer be at the whims of people and situations. At some point in this book you will get the 'a ha' that will transform your current challenges into vehicles for more success and happiness.

No, you can't stop the cycle from rising and falling but like a wave you can learn how to surf it. And if you do you will almost instantly begin to see a new and higher vision of yourself and start to achieve more with less time and effort.

All it will take is a bit of courage. Do you have enough courage to read this book? Are you worthy of all the benefits that this book might bring you?

That question probably makes you squirm in your chair a bit. I hope it does. That's the first step.

You are about to embark on the same journey I started almost twenty years ago during my dark nights of the soul. I am certain the answers I arrived at along the way will help you rise into a Higher Self that can manifest whatever it desires.

With Gratitude,

Allan Hunkin

Thought Leaders Who Have Influenced This Work

Chuck Spezzano Psych Of Vision	Teertha Mistlberger Website
Joe Vitale Attract Money Now	Shelora Fitzgerald Website
Sandy Levey On Purpose	Zig Ziglar Website
Duane O'Kane ClearMind Inst	John Bradshaw Website

TABLE OF CONTENTS

Publisher Information 2
- *Other books by Allan Hunkin:* *3*
- *Early praise for 'Your Worthiness Cycle'* *4*
- *Dedication* *5*
- *My Sincere Appreciation* *6*

Introduction 7
- *Definitions - The Worthiness Cycle Model* *13*

Resources for Expanding Worthiness 15
- *Your Worthiness Cycle DVD* *15*
- *Talks and Keynotes* *16*
- *Seminars and Workshops* *16*
- *Coaching and Counseling* *16*
- *Consulting* *16*
- *The Need For Speed* *17*
  - Worthiness Quotient Evaluation and Assessment 17
- *Customized and Bulk Book Orders* *17*

Your Worthiness Cycle 18
- *Is this the right book for you today?* *18*

The Worthiness Cycle Model of Empowerment 19
  - How The Worthiness Cycle Came To Be 19
  - One Picture is Worth a Thousand Words 20
- *The Importance of Worthiness in Our Lives* *21*
  - Why haven't you heard about Worthiness before? 21
  - Strong Forces Work Against Our Success 22
- *That Which Is Not Measured Does Not Exist* *23*
  - A Lot Is Going On At All Times 24
  - Feelings and Emotions Play an Important Role 24
  - Our Brain's Connections Networks 24
  - Our Perceptions of Situations and Events 25
  - The Past Becomes The Future 25
  - The Most Innocent Mistake We Make 26
- *What Does the Worthiness Cycle Measure?* *26*
  - There is Too Much to Measure 26
  - Bringing Everything Together 27

Worthiness In The 21st Century 28
- *Worthiness: The Quantum View* *28*
- *Worthiness: The Up Close and Personal View* *28*
  - Be a Fly On The Wall in The Mall 29
  - Everyone Has An Abundance Threshold (AT) 30
  - Our Eyes Are The Windows Of The Soul 30
  - Mr. Z and Me 32
  - All Progress is Deeply Personal 33
- *Our Journey Towards True Innocence and Value* *33*

Your Journey Begins 34
The Most Important Decision You Will Make........................... 34
    The Question 34
    The Case for Evil is Loud and Overwhelming..................... 34
    The Case For Innocence Speaks Softly 35
    The Choice 35
    Choosing Evil 35
    Choosing Innocence 36
    There Is No 'Maybe '... 36
    A Deeper Connection 36
Connection and Fulfillment 36
    Worthiness Is The Gatekeeper 37
Intelligence in the 21st Century.. 38
Connectedness - Our Deepest Desire 39
Fulfillment of Our Dreams, Desires and Purpose..................... 40
Worthiness is By Nature Holistic 41
    Hiding From Happiness.. 42
    You Can't Hide Half A Thought!... 42
    Worthiness – A Universal Phenomena 42
What Gets In Our Way? 42
    Living Immersed in Conflicting Needs 43
    Our Basic Needs 43
    Judgments 44
    Polarizations 45
    Duality 45
    Duality And Our Constructs Of Reality 45
The Need For A Single Theme and Pattern.............................. 46

The Four Quadrants Of Fulfillment 48
    Our Outer Journey - Quadrants One & Two 48
        Going Out And Getting 48
        Going Out And Giving 48
    Our Inner Journey - Quadrants Three & Four 49
        Going Within and Allowing.. 49
        Remaining Within and Receiving....................................... 49
    What Do We Know About Receiving?..................................... 50
        "It is better to give than to receive." 50
        The Four Quadrants Combined 50
    Definitions of a Cycle... 50
        Your Unique Worthiness Cycle 51
    Direction Indicators... 52
        The Space Between Your Thoughts 52
        Worthiness Cycle Timeframes 53
        Learn Your Trigger Points 53
        The Truth is Always Positive 54
        All Worthiness is in the 'Now'.. 54
        From Reaction to Observation 55

Your Worthiness Cycle Step By Step 56
First Step: Learn To Be The Observer On Demand 56
Life's Ups and Downs 57
Our Life's Time Line 57
We want Abundance and we want it now! 58
The Worthiness Arena 59
Your Worthiness Setpoint (WSP) 60
- How Good Can I Stand It? 61
- How Bad Will I Let It Get? 61
Self Esteem, Self Worth and Worthiness 62
The Gravitational Pull of Worthiness Setpoint 63
- Viewing Needs, Polarity and Duality Differently 63
- Our Abundance Allowance Range 64
- Unrealized' Worthiness 64
More Receiving (MOR) 64
Heading Up To 'Everything' 65
The Fear / Attractiveness Dynamic 65
Then Something Happens! 67
Life Should Be Better Than This! 68
Our Second Greatest Fear (2GF) 70
- 'Everything' is Greater Than 'Nothing' 70
- The Different Feelings Above and Below Our WSP 71
- Emotional Heat 71
- Don't Get Too Abundant and Make God Mad 71
- "Oh My God!" 72
Our Single Greatest Fear (1GF) 72
- Our Worthiness Cycle is Life Long 74
Addiction – The Opposite of Abundance 75
- Choice points 75
Allowing Ever Increasing Abundance 76
- Abundance Anxiety (AA) 77
- Worthiness And Relationships 77
Mistakes That Cost Us Our Life 77

The NOT So Comfortable Zone 79
- The Comfort Zone 79
- The Control Zone 80
- The Dead Zone 80
- High Effort and Energy Demand 80
- On the Menu Tonight 'Deep Fried Human' 81
- Never Take Your Eyes Off The Prize 81
Insisting on Being Right 82
Keeping Ourselves Safe and Small 83
- Gathered Evidence to Support Discomfort 83
- Get Familiar, Comfortable And Confident 84
- Survival, Safety and Conquest 85
Worthiness Meltdowns 86

  A Worthiness Meltdown Step By Step 87
  Meltdown Stems From Our 'Fear of Greatness' 88
 Counter Balancers to Worthiness *88*

Core Principles of Worthiness 90

Everything Wants To Live For Ever *90*
Life is a Cycle Not A Struggle *91*
We Are Committed To Both Success and Failure *92*
  The Games of Failure and Success 93
  The Game of 'Almost' 94
Receiving Is The Greatest Giving of All *96*
  Achievement More And Then More Again 96
Connection to 'Everything' is our only Desire *98*

What Impacts Your Worthiness Quotient 99

Things that Affects Your Worthiness Quotient *99*
  Outer versus Inner World Persona 99
  Your Universal Bank Account 100
  Our Perceptions of What Happened 101
  Subjective Versus Objective 102
  The Past Is Never Really The Past 103
  Fear Causes Change of Direction 103
What You Feed Expands *104*
Be Aware The Soft Voice *105*

The Way Back to Abundance 106

15 Ways to Gain Access to Worthiness *106*
Our Feelings Tell Us Where We Are *107*
  Letting Go and Unlearning 107
  How long is all this going to take? 107
  The Fastest Way to 'Everything' 108
  Have you sinned or made mistake? 108
  Transforming into Good 109
  An 'In Person' Forgiveness Scenario 110
Be Out Ahead *111*
  Awareness 111
  Commitment 112
  A Deal is a Deal 113
What is non-negotiable for you? *114*
  Action 114
  Get Out Of The Details 114

Upping Your Worthiness Quotient 115

Things I Overheard While Out Walking With Myself *115*
  Words Tell Us The Thoughts We Are Thinking. 115
Finding Your Trigger Points *116*
  Time Link 118
  Remember to Ask Yourself Questions 119
  Hello eMaEo 119

A Good Friend of Yours	119
"Why am I creating this NOW?"	120
Measurement Doesn't Exist In 'Everything'	*120*
Upward And Onward	*121*
You're on your way!	*121*

Bibliography 123
Additional Resources 123

The Life Enrichment Series	*123*
Other books in the series:	*123*
Teaching The Worthiness Cycle to People We Care About	*123*
Your Situation is Unique	*124*
I want to work with you personally.	125
Three Step Counseling / Coaching Sources	*125*
How to Get Started?	125
About Allan Hunkin	*126*

Definitions - The Worthiness Cycle Model

"How bad will I Let it Get?" - The territory below our initial Worthiness Setpoint.

"I want to be right!" - The program running in our mind that keeps us in the Control Zone.

"If I just do one thing wrong" - The theme of the anxiety we experience above our Thriving Line.

"Life should be better than this"- The theme of the worry we experience below our Surviving Line.

1GF - The number one fear we encounter on our way to Everything,

2GF - The second greatest fear that keeps us from going beyond Nothing.

Abundance - The experience of an appropriate amount of excess that doesn't take away from others' Abundance.

Abundance Anxiety (AA) - Abundance Anxiety is something we experience when we are receiving more attention, riches, love than we are able to take in without losing control of the situation and being completely overwhelmed.

Comfort Zone - The distance we have risen and fallen from our original Setpoint.

Control Zone - Our attempt to regulate the distance we travel in life by staying in our Comfort Zone.

Dead Zone - The final stage of existence in our Comfort Zone where we have become numb, and unmotivated.

eMaEo (pronounced 'me') - eMaEo sands for 'easing More and Everything out'. It is the rebel part of our mind does not want us to succeed at anything.

Everything - A realm of light within the mind where total Connectedness, Abundance and Fulfillment resides.

Everything Good - A place just before Everything.

Failure - A master program in our minds, with many sub-programs, that is constantly heading us towards Nothing.

FEAR - Forget Everything And Run.

HBD - stands for 'How Bad Will I Let It Get?" which is all territory below our original Worthiness Setpoint.

HGD - stands for 'How Good Can You Stand It" and is all territory above our initial Worthiness Setpoint.

Layer – A layer of fear, shame, guilt that we created as a result of hurts, wounds and negative experiences

MO (pronounced 'm oh') - MO stands for the 'Momentum we have On the Worthiness Cycle.

MOR - stands for More Receiving and is the name given to the neural network in our mind that, when active, causes us to move forward and upwards in the Worthiness Cycle. It is our attraction to Everything and Nothing and our experience in life of everything in between.

NEED - stands for 'Never Ending Emotional Demands.' It is the program used by eMaEo to have us justify why we are showing up in the world in a way contrary to MOR.

NOMOR - Current location in the Worthiness Cycle indicating our current degree of Worthiness.

Nothing - The realm of denseness where Numbness, Meaningless and Valuelessness resides.

Our Worthiness Quotient - Our current capacity to receive and allow ourselves to benefit from life's abundant offerings no matter the category, intensity and duration.

***Our Worthiness Setpoint* (WSP)** - The anchor point we've established within the Worthiness arena. It is the location where we feel the safest.

Surviving Line - Our Worthiness Setpoint and threshold at the lower edge of our Comfort Zone.

Success - A master program in our mind, with many sub-programs, that points us towards Everything.

The Worthiness Cycle - Contained in the mind The Worthiness Cycle is the primary cycle everyone travels throughout life in search of Success, Fulfillment, Connection and Love.

The Worthiness Model - The name given to the container for all of the elements of Worthiness as it is presented within Cycle.

Thriving Line - Our Worthiness Setpoint at the upper edge of our Comfort Zone.

Worthiness - A state within us where we completely accept our innate innocence and infinite value no matter what we have said, done, experienced or observed.

Worthiness Filter - Mental lenses through which you measure degree of Innocence and Value including and against your own

Resources for Expanding Worthiness

Your Worthiness Cycle DVD

'Your Worthiness Cycle DVD' is a 55 minute audio/visual companion to the book that explains the Worthiness Cycle step by step.

Produced and narrated by the creator *'Your Worthiness Cycle DVD'* covers each section of the book plus more on how the Worthiness Cycle applies to Relationship, Parenting, Health, Wellness as well as Work, Career, Organization and Teams.

Team Leaders, Consultant, Coaches Relationship Counselors will discover that' Your Worthiness Cycle DVD' is a highly effective way of providing Worthiness principles and technique. The DVD is a way of explaining to family members, the benefits of learning and understanding Worthiness no matter whether they have reading the book. not. For athletes, sport teams wanting to improve their overall performance to student wanting better grades 'Your Worthiness Cycle DVD' is an valuable resource.

Talks and Keynotes

Worthiness is a key ingredient of Success and applicable to everyone. Worthiness, as Allan Hunkin explains it, is holistic and is located way deeper than either our self-esteem or self-worth. Although practically invisible it plays an ever expanding and important role in our Achievements, Happiness and Fulfillment in the 21st Century.

Allan Hunkin's approach to Worthiness is the result of over eighteen years of research and has never been presented before now in this way. Each and every attendee will really value learning how Worthiness works, both for and against them, in their work, relationships and health and longevity.

Allan Hunkin has been speaking for over thirty years. He is guaranteed to have attendees laughing and really enjoying themselves, while at the same time learning ways to expand their Worthiness in all aspects of their personal/professional life.

Worthiness – The Key to Success, Happiness and Fulfillment is totally fresh and unique. No speaker today offers this important topic.

Worthiness – The Key to Success, Happiness and Fulfillment addresses career, relationships. and the world in which we live. Techniques for improving our worthiness quotient are an important part of this highly informative and professionally delivered talk. Because Worthiness affects us all in everything we do Allan is able to tailor each keynote and/or breakout at the event.

Seminars and Workshops

Allan conducts seminars and workshops on Worthiness for corporations and organizations large and small. Custom tailored for each client he seminar is 3 hours and the workshop is a full day.

Coaching and Counseling

Having graduated from the ClearMind Institute Allan is a trained councilor with thirty plus years of personal development experience He holds 'train the trainer' status in five different models of personal empowerment. Allan counsels both individuals and couples in creating breakthroughs for the challenges they are currently facing.

Consulting

Does your organization or team need a fresh perspective in order to really 'go for it'? Do some projects seem to go south for no visible or logical reason? Consulting to businesses and organizations, both large and small, has been is a key aspect of Allan's work for many years.

The Need For Speed

Within any group working on projects there are some that are working hard to succeed and exceed expectations. Some are openly resistant and impede progress. Individuals, within a smaller group, have a negative impact throughout the project because sub-consciously they are working against early completions and exceeded performance and results.

All three groups, to a greater or lesser degree have a fear of being overwhelmed with too much progress and success. Leaders who can identify and reduce the degree of this hidden drag on progress will deliver better results in less time and cost.

Worthiness Quotient Evaluation and Assessment

Each assignment starts with a full and in-dept assessment. The goal is to help management identify where individuals and groups are working against progress on any given project. The on sight assessment and consulting provides leaders and senior management with tools and techniques to identify earlier performance issue as a result of a low Worthiness Quotient of individuals and groups.

Customized and Bulk Book Orders

The book 'Your Worthiness Cycle' is available for bulk purchase. The book cover and some content can be customized for any organization's professional development needs.

Your Worthiness Cycle

A Breakthrough Method to Unleash Your Power to Manifest The Life You've Always Wanted

Is this the right book for you today?

10 questions in no particular order that will indicate whether any of this book applies to you.

1. Do you often feel like you are on a rollercoaster, experiencing more ups and downs than other people you know?
2. Do you feel that life has been a real struggle and more than you thought it would be? Shouldn't life be better than this?
3. Do you feel like you are bogged down and that life is somewhat dull and even boring sometimes?
4. Are you abundant in the areas of money, career, relationships, health? In which are you the most abundant and which one do you have the least?
5. Do projects, opportunities and relationships you're involved in seem to unexpectedly go wrong, get off track or melt away all together. Do you seem to hear about opportunities later than you need to, to take advantage of them?
6. How successful have you been at winning against your addictions, and other self-sabotaging themes and patterns that are getting in the way of your Success and Happiness?
7. Have you been prone to accidents, mix ups, worry, anxiety, drama, bad luck? Do you have a tendency to "Buy High and Sell Low?"
8. Do you have people in your life holding you back but you can't bring yourself to move on?
9. Do you feel there is something, that you've never been able to identify, working hard at having you fail rather than succeed?
10. What people and situations have you put into your life that are 'protecting' you from having to deal with Success?

If any of these ring true for you then you are only pages away from answers you may have been seeking for a long time.

The Worthiness Cycle Model of Empowerment

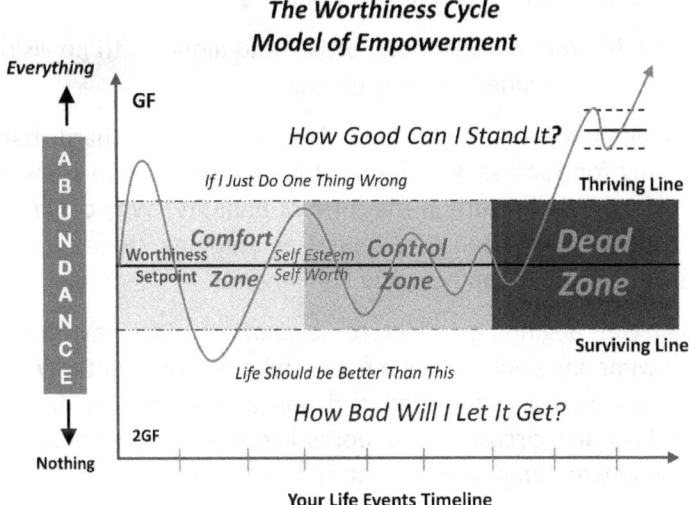

How The Worthiness Cycle Came To Be

In the spring of 1991, I had run out of rabbits to pull out of the hat, and I needed some answers. "Why has my life become such a roller-coaster of ups and downs?" I asked myself. I had built a half a dozen interesting businesses to various levels of success, but somehow they had all ended up not paying off in any meaningful way.

I had been a guy that had really 'gone for it'. I had read the personal growth books and taken all the seminars. I had been teaching personal development for several years, but none of that had its intended effect.

In the last six months of that year, I went through bankruptcy, Cancer, and divorce. The radiation left me unable to climb a set of stairs without going sheet white and almost getting sick to my stomach. I sat alone in a room for most of that six months asking myself "how the hell did I get here?"

I embarked on a deep and personal healing journey unlike anything I had ever undertaken before. If I was going to bother to make another attempt at having a successful life, I wanted to know what was at the core of my many failures. I pulled myself apart at the seams.

Up until that time, I had invested all my self-education in learning how to 'go out and get' what I wanted out of life. 'Go for it' was my rallying cry to myself and everyone around me.

Now, at age 38 I found myself sick, broke, and alone, with no vision of the future that included a happy ending.

The dominant question in my mind was "after all this hard, hard work, striving for Success, why hadn't I been able to have some of the energy expended return in the form of benefits? Why couldn't I gain a foothold that lasted and served as stepping stones to the next level of Success, Happiness and Fulfillment?"

By 1994, I was beginning to get some answers. One day, sitting around a swimming pool helping a friend, who had momentarily lost his way, I grabbed a yellow pad and pen and started to draw a bunch of lines and circles. "It all works like this," I explained, not knowing what was going to come out of my mouth next.

Twenty minutes later, what you are going to see visually presented throughout this book had made its way onto my yellow pad. Reviewing what I had drawn a few hours later, I was startled to realize how many answers I had myself in such a short period of time.

On that warm sunny day I began, what has turned out to be an eighteen-year quest, to understand and explain the answers that poured out onto a few pages in a matter of a minutes. I really haven't added much to this way of looking at Worthiness over the last eighteen years but I have found better and better ways of explaining it.

One Picture is Worth a Thousand Words

The Worthiness Cycle represented throughout this book is a visual mode. The image above represents the whole model. Beginning with the line at the bottom that goes from left to right and the line to the left, which goes up and down, we are going to explore Worthiness characteristic upon characteristic. My goal is to make what has been invisible to most of us visible.

Take time to study and consider each of the graphic representations. Like many deep things, the revelations come layer by layer. For many people the validity and value of each graphic is not always immediately evident so don't start beating yourself up if you're 'not getting it' right away.

The Worthiness Cycle is an abstract idea of something that is very real in everyone's life. At first glance, the model might seem a bit too left brained/linier but that in fact is an important part of its value. The up and down cycle line represents how much of our Worthiness we have access to at any specific point in the cycle.

Each point in the cycle represents a place filled with emotions, fear, anxiety, heartbreak, gratitude, joy, successes, and failures. Make no mistake about it. Cerebral or not, every time you go through the cycle, any expansion that causes you to rise will be hard won wisdom requiring a lot of awareness, understanding and mindfulness. The parts of us that hide our true Worthiness don't give it up just by being asked.

Having said that you will need to invest some mind time looking at the visuals and letting them tell you 'your story.' You should not take everything presented here as the Gospel according to Allan Hunkin. Worthiness consists of basic themes and recurring patterns that are expressed in ways that are unique to each of us. Naturally, they will occur somewhat differently in your life than the formula presented in the book.

The Importance of Worthiness in Our Lives

Most people don't have a clue what Worthiness is, and even less of an idea of how important it is to living a meaningful, fulfilling life.

After a several years of research, combined with the hard won wisdom of my own personal experience, I have come to know that Worthiness is absolutely and vitally important to our success. I can state the following without hesitation:

- Worthiness is the gatekeeper to everything good that will ever happen to us or be accomplished by us.
- Worthiness is the most important thing we will ever learn about ourselves and others.

Why haven't you heard about Worthiness before?

By the end of this book you will most likely agree that knowing and understanding your Worthiness Cycle is a key step in realizing your full potential. Given that the two statements above are true, why haven't you heard more about it before now? Here are a few of the reasons:

- There has been very little written about Worthiness from the perspective presented here.

- Worthiness, with all its ups and downs, is too vast a subject to try and explain in words alone. It requires some kind of visual model to represent its complexity. The model I've developed provides us with an easy way to both see and understand Worthiness.
- You were never taught the real meaning of it and how it affects our life.
- Even if you ended up with an innate sense of your own worthiness there is almost nothing about daily living that will lift your worthiness level. In fact, it's the opposite. Just showing up for life, as we have set it up, is a worthiness-robbing experience.
- Even if nothing negative happens to you, your worthiness quotient will gradually drop lower and lower until the thought of living longer is not a positive thought and then you depart for places unknown. And the awareness of our brothers from the East isn't much better... sitting cross-legged on a mountain top and chanting to your second chakra will have very limited affect.
- Up until now you were never given a model or method for expanding your worthiness quotient.

Strong Forces Work Against Our Success

As soon as you begin to rise in your worthiness cycle the part of you that 'doesn't want you to be successful' kicks in and, without some awareness knowledge and skills, talks you out of making the most positive choice.

Review your life achievements versus what you thought you were going to achieve. The broken dreams, goals and relationships left in your wake says that, without fresh awareness and skills to counter this, changing direction is a very difficult task.

We all have the same dilemma no matter what level we are at. How do we convince ourselves to put in the effort to expand our worthiness levels if we, deep inside, don't feel worthy of the benefits of an expanded worthiness?

Without an awareness of this dynamic:

- You won't buy or finish books that will impact you in the most positive ways.
- You won't take the seminars, workshops, counseling and coaching that you 'really' need.

- You won't bring into your life people with knowledge and experience who will help expand your awareness. In fact you'll bring people who distract you from it.

- You won't be home when Abundance comes knocking, because if you were you'd bump into Ease, Flow, Success and Happiness which would then expand your worthiness capability even more.

Becoming aware of our Worthiness Cycle and how it work for and against us takes commitment, focus and dedication to the practice of allowing yourself to see what your mind has you convinced that you can't see.

There are several subtle differences between seeing, understanding and actually getting ahead of our own Worthiness scotoma (blind spots). The minute you have embodied the basic principles you'll see dozens of ways how you can use the Worthiness Cycle as a tool for creating the life you know is possible.

> *"Worthiness is a state within where our built up resistance to Success, Happiness and Fulfillment is no longer in control."*

That Which Is Not Measured Does Not Exist

The human body has 26 organs and gland systems that are all constantly having an effect on each other. Some have an effect on primarily only one system while others have an effect on several. All combined have an effect on the whole system. When some are rising in importance others are subsiding, depending upon the body and mind's requirements to maintain strength, endurance and the ability to repair itself. All of these reactions are caused by the environmental conditions that are being experienced moment by moment in our exterior world.

One of the easiest examples is our adrenal glands. Adrenaline is released from the adrenal glands when the body believes it is involved in a stressful situation. In fact, we're designed so that our bodies even build up adrenaline levels in anticipation of danger. This adrenaline rush prepares the body for what we call "fight or flight." With a rush of adrenaline, your heart rate and breathing rate increases and your senses become more acute. Your eyes see more clearly. Your brain thinks more clearly, readying the body for flight. Nutrients are released to sustain muscular activity and blood flow is regulated away from less important organs to the muscles to prepare for a fight. The body keeps up this preparation until it no longer feels threatened. All of this happens within a couple of seconds.

A Lot Is Going On At All Times

For a simple calculation, if you split the total number of organs and glands into groups of 13 and 13 there are **6,227,020,800** permutations, or 'combinations of effects' within the organ and gland system. Every one of these permutations causes different physiological responses which affect our feelings, emotions and states.

Feelings and Emotions Play an Important Role

There are over 1000 feelings and emotions that we can have. We all experience 25 or more each day. Multiplying 1000 to the number of organ and glandular permutations, (6,227,020,800 X 1,000) = I have no earthly idea... a whole bunch!

According to Deepak Chopra we have at least 60,000 thoughts a day. Take the first bunch arrived at above and multiply by 60,000 and you get an even bigger bunch.

Our Brain's Connections Networks

Your brain consists of about 100 billion neurons and there are anywhere from 1,000 to 10,000 synapses for each neuron. (100 Fascinating Facts You Never Knew About the Human Brain)

The neural networks of our brain and central nervous system are comparable to, but infinitely more sophisticated than the fiber-optic network connecting millions of computers together in a single network that we have come to know as the Internet.

One main difference is that instead of millions of computers our brain has up to 100 billion "computers", (neurons), connected together in a biological network that is much more than 10,000 times a system like AT&T.

And, just like the Internet, our brain has networks... embedded in networks... embedded in networks... and so on.

A neural network is a cluster of neurons connected together to form a "database" of encoded information such as thoughts, feelings, beliefs, programmed reactions, emotions and even physiological data. Neural networks are the actual biological location of change. Change does not take place without re-wiring of existing neural connections or creating entirely new connections. This is why we literally 'become what we think about most of the time.' (Carter)

Our Perceptions of Situations and Events

Every second your entire life your body and mind are going through billions of changes. These accumulate to form our perceptions of events and situations we are experiencing in the present moment.

Our perceptions are also being influenced greatly by our memory of *'how'* we perceived similar situations experienced in the past, whether they were real or imagined.

> *"Of all the thoughts you could be thinking why are you thinking the thoughts your thinking?"*
>
> ~ Dr. Chuck Spezzano

The Past Becomes The Future

All of these combinations generate feedback loops to tell us to do more, less or avoid each opportunity that presents itself to us.

Based upon our past experiences and, *'what'* we decided those experiences meant, we mistakenly start to avoid things that look similar but are now good for us at this moment in our life.

Because the mind doesn't see what it has been instructed to ignore we can easily make choices that cause us to change direction on a path that is leading us in a positive direction and hurry away from the very things that would provide us more success, happiness and abundance.

Even worse, we won't even know it has happened until we are thirty minutes, thirty miles or thirty years down the road when those choices have created situations so counter productive that they are now causing us great pain and loss rather than pleasure and happiness. *(The objective of this book is to help you learn how to become aware that you have turned away from Abundance in 30 seconds or less.)*

The result... feelings of shame and guilt, for not making better choices produce regret, that often does not dissipate in our lifetime. As we look back and do a life review we are usually shocked at all the carnage we have inflicted on ourselves and others.

Guilt, shame and regret are the lowest vibrations we can experience as human beings. (David R. Hawkins) They progressively drain us of our life force and our will to keep going.

Many longevity experts tell us that we could be living to about 140 years old before we expire. But we only live to be about *'half'* that. It is this unhealed shame that causes our early death, *'with most of our music still in us.'* We die because we have never learned how to unload all the shame, guilt and fear so the thought of living decades longer is just too much to bare.

The Most Innocent Mistake We Make

This is a totally innocent mistake. We don't come equipped with an onboard system that provides us with an awareness of how this dynamic affects us so there is no way that we can be aware, in advance of its affect, on our success throughout life. We only begin to become aware of this of when we start to experience the negative affects of these mistaken choices.

We are innocent as newborn babies here nevertheless, most human beings, make an even bigger mistake next. We decided that *'we'* are to blame and because we look for someone to blame we decide that our parents, and those that did us harm are also guilty. We mistakenly decide that we must be flawed in some way or we were born guilty and therefore we are being punished for something, but we have no idea what that is.

No matter how hard we search, how many self help books, seminars and/or counseling sessions we consume there seems to be no logical answer. The next mistake... the only answer must be that 'God' must be punishing us. Every one of these decisions cause a chance in direction or momentum in your worthiness cycle.

What Does the Worthiness Cycle Measure?
There is Too Much to Measure

How can you measure every one of these biological, physiological and psychological permutations that influence your choices and form your perceptions? The answer is *'you can't'*, you never could and never will. It is absolutely impossible. This is all too much for us to consciously be aware of what's going on and how to change it.

You can't measure the impact of all these combinations but you can combine all of them into one overall holistic measurement that helps you recognize much sooner whether you are heading towards your own particular version of heaven or hell.'

Bringing Everything Together

In allowing our brain/mind to morph all this data, (much of it conflicting), into one up and down cycle we employ our mind's vast capability to do all the calculating and combine everything into something we can begin to grasp. influence. With practice, we can gain the ability to cause positive outcomes consistently and much sooner than we would have.

The Worthiness Cycle model combines all the biological, physiological and psychological changes that constitute the cycles of life, into one over-arching cycle, that is relevant to everyday living. With it we can then influence the direction of our lives towards our higher pursuits of Connection and Fulfillment.

Perhaps you are now beginning to understand why I wrote earlier... *"Worthiness is the gatekeeper to everything good that will ever happen to us or be accomplished by us."* and *"Worthiness is the most important thing we will ever learn about ourselves and others."*

> *"All men should strive to learn before they die,*
> *what they are running from, and to, and why."*
> *~ James Thurber*

> Sometimes, you find yourself in the middle of nowhere, and sometimes, in the middle of nowhere, you find yourself.

Worthiness In The 21st Century

"Everything comes from everything, and everything is made out of everything, and everything returns into everything."

~Leonardo Da Vinci

Worthiness: The Quantum View

How many of these statements can you can allow to be true?

1. The Universe is made up of energy and information which forms into denser partials known as atoms. (Deepak Chopra)
2. Every atom in the Universe is equal to every other atom and has the potential to become anything and everything.
3. Every atom is of innate value, completely integral therefore worthy of becoming anything and everything.
4. Every atom is worthy so Worthiness is an integral part of everything and represents full and total Potentiality.
5. As Worthiness is Everything then Everything is Worthiness.
6. You are made up of atoms and each and every atom you are made of is worthy.
7. Worthiness is all pervasive. It is a fact, a complete, holistic truth about ourselves,
8. Therefore we are worthy and worthy of Everything.

Worthiness: The Up Close and Personal View

When you ask people if they are worthy most will answer with a strong *"yes, of course."*

Often the first things that come to mind are external to us... a good job, a loving partner, a flashy car, winning the Lotto. Fundamentally it is true. We *'are'* worthy of this and every other good thing that life offers up to us.

I used to have a radio show called "*How Good Can You Stand It?*' and would ask people all the time... 'How good can YOU stand it?'

Most everyone responds with a nudge, nudge, wink, wink, a smile and says: *"oh I can assure you. I can stand it REAL good!"*

Most of us believe we can handle lots of good things happening to us. Most of us believe we can handle a lot of good things happening all at the same time and/or one right after the other, in rapid succession.

Be a Fly On The Wall in The Mall

Let's do a little hidden camera experiment. Let's say you are both walking down the hall in a shopping mall and at the same time you are with me in a separate room watching us both via a remote video camera.

You notice I'm seated at an unassuming table in your path. There are no signs or anything to tell you who I am or why I am there. With a friendly smile on my face I beckon you over and invite you to take just a moment and see what I am offering.

You decided to risk the stop. After all, you decide, how much trouble can this guy cause... he's smiling and there's nothing on the table to indicate I am going to be talked into buying another high powered juicer, 'guaranteed not to rust, bust or collect dust.'

Without giving you any good reason for why I am doing it I ask you to open your hand. I begin laying $100 bills into your palm one after the other.

"One hundred... two hundred.... three hundred"

You laugh a short laugh and look around to see who's watching and you blurt out *"Wow... great. What's this all about?"*

"No reason... "it's a gift with no future obligation whatsoever... four hundred... five hundred.... six hundred...

You laugh again but this time it is nervous laugh. *"Hey what do I have to do for this money?"* you ask sheepishly. "*I repeat... Nothing!.* It's a gift with no future obligation whatsoever." seven hundred... eight hundred... nine hundred."

You might make a move to walk away but I just look into your eyes, smile a reassuring smile. And, I keep going but this time I double the amount... *"eleven hundred... thirteen hundred.... fifteen hundred..."*

Then with no advance warning I increase the amount again... *"twenty five hundred... thirty five hundred... forty-five hundred..."*

Everyone Has An Abundance Threshold (AT)

I don't know when the stress goes over the top and you get afraid and anxious and you say something like *"Wait a minute... you have to tell me why you are doing this and what am I now obligated to do for this money!"* Possibly you will just close your hand walk away quickly. You might even put all the money back on the table and make a bee-line for the door.

Now you can say that you wouldn't get anxious, angry and afraid but we all know inside that there is a moment and a number, at which point you must get away from this instant abundance, at least until you find out exactly how much of your soul you have to sell to keep the money.

Given enough time I know I could reveal what things you run away from. There is a place where you will not only run away from things like Fame, Wealth, Achievement, Fame, but also from internal things like higher amounts of Kindness, Affection, Appreciation, Sex, Intimacy and Love. Success and Intimacy rank high on the list.

No matter what its is we all have a threshold with everything, external or internal. There is a line, above which we become increasingly anxious and afraid, as we rise higher and higher above it. In the Worthiness Cycle model this is call this your **'Thriving Line.'**

Our Eyes Are The Windows Of The Soul

Let's try another example. Let's say you've been invited over to a friend's place along with a number of other people you know who are also friends. You trust, for the most part, everyone in the room. You are warm, dry, fed, safe, and well liked as well, by everyone present.

Your friend proposes an exercise where you are to pick someone at random and sit opposite to them and look into their eyes while thinking loving thoughts towards them for as long as you can without thinking about something else. The objective is to see how long you can look directly into their eyes before you look away for some reason.

You find yourself sitting in front of one of the most beautiful people you have ever come in contact with. Over the course of a fifteen minutes conversation, getting to know each other, you realize that this person loves you very much, not in a romantic way, but simply 'for who you are.'

The exercise begins. You start to look into your partner's eyes with as much of a loving a gaze as you can find within yourself. You begin to feel their love radiating out of them in abundance, without judgment or restraint. You feel this Love penetrating you like never before.

As the connection between you grows their love begins to build within you. Along with this love thoughts and memories begin to stir within you. Some are memories of where you loved and you loved well. Some are where you came up short. A few are thoughts where you said you would 'be there' for someone and you weren't. Circumstances were beyond your control. Several of the most intense thoughts and memories are of where you went against your word and weren't there when you said you would and, you made that choice deliberately.

If you maintain your loving gaze for ninety seconds, before looking away, you are very much the exception, not the rule. A group of practitioners, skilled in every aspect of this exercise took more than two years of continuous practice to be able to reach 90 seconds without being over powered by the need to break the connection, look away and interrupt the 'receiving.'

Think about this for a moment. This exercise was with someone you didn't even know. Imagine how difficult it would be if you knew the person and knew that they did in fact love you unconditionally. Imagine your world if you were able to double your ability to actually, authentically receive and allow yourself the benefits of deep connections and Love. Imagine if the people you are sharing life with could do the same.

Some people seem to be able to maintain their loving gazes for longer but this is because they are not 'really' connecting with the other person or letting the other person's love reach into them. They are pretending to be connected but actually have erected a virtual wall to 'protect' themselves. They do this because, having been abandoned before, they don't believe that the Love is real and/or will be taken away without notice *'again.'*

These walls, that every one of us have, are there to keep our judgments, needs, fears inside because they 'make us able to cope with loss. But, the walls are there also to save us from receiving the love that is being offered' which we 'know' we don't deserve because of something we are ashamed of and are keeping secret from everyone.

Mr. Z and Me

For several years, when I lived in an apartment next to the airport in Vancouver, I had a big male, white haired cat named Mr. Z.

Every day at around 4:00pm I would try to get down for a nap. No matter where he was in the apartment or how 'asleep' he was at the time he would somehow know I had laid down and within two minutes, he would hop up onto my bed and then plop himself on my chest and lay down.

I developed a ritual over time of a scratch behind one ear, then the other, then the chin, then in the pit under each of his two front paws, etc. I loved this crazy cat. I took care to do the ritual always the same so that he would trust me, love me and enjoy it even more.

It took me two years to get him to let me include rubbing his eyes ever so gently with the back of my finger. He had trusted me everywhere else but eventually he decided that the eye rub was the best part and would push his face right against my finger and purr like a Bengal tiger when we came to that part.

I would conk off and wake up anywhere from 30 to 45 minutes later. Mr. Z would be sprawled out on my chest, fast asleep, completely dead to the world and I'd often have to wake him so I could get up. I grew to love Mr. Z more than any other being on the planet. I'm pretty sure the feelings were mutual.

Sometimes I would awaken and he would be lying with his head on his two front paws just looking at me which he would continue to do for several minutes.

Somewhere along the way I decided to return his loving gaze and do some things deliberately as a way of getting to know Mr. Z and myself at deeper and deeper levels. First I would look into his eyes and gently broadcast loving thoughts in his direction. Second I would, as much as I possibly could, allow the full extent of his love to flow into my eyes without restriction. I trained myself to open and receive his love to the depth that I could find was possible for me.

I trained myself to notice when I felt anxious for some reason, then to identify what it was I was being anxious about. It was always about guilt, fear, shame, abandonment and/or a belief about myself that I was putting out into the world in the form of judgment onto others.

Through mindfulness I learned how to just 'allow' those thoughts without trying to push them away and at the same time continue to open and connect to the truth of the love that Mr. Z had for me. Even still I'm sure I never got to a full minute without having to turn away, squelch my anxiousness and catch my spiritual breath.

One thing that always interrupted the connection and flow was if I needed Mr. Z to react to me and show me that he loved me in some way. Whenever I thought that I needed more of his love he would become bored and hop off the bed, leaving me feeling even more needy and abandoned.

A large component of Worthiness is understanding shame, guilt, abandonment and fear and how to release yourself from their grip so you can rise higher each time in your Worthiness Cycle. **Needs** (which I call '***Never Ending Emotional Demands***') always interrupt connection and flow.

All Progress is Deeply Personal

I learned a lot about my own Worthiness from Mr. Z because I allowed it to become 'personal.' I made it my own. I committed to receiving. It's fine to say that you would never walk away from a guy in a mall handing you hundred dollar bills or turn away from someone who is looking at you in a deeply loving way but what about the love that comes at you that you can't control. Total Abundance and the Love you can't control is called '***Everything'*** in the Worthiness Cycle model.

Our Journey Towards True Innocence and Value

If you eventually allow yourself to receive true innocence, you will undoubtedly have your '*come to Jesus moment*.' This experience, of our true innocence and value, might have lasted only half a second but, it is a game changer. No matter how long it lasted it launches us on a quest to experience it again and again with increasingly intensity and frequency. (In the worthiness cycle model is represented when you are heading up in the cycle.)

> "*Our healing and changes do not happen in steps like a ladder. They happen in spirals and layers*"
>
> ~ SARK

Your Journey Begins

This path is different for everyone but it always involves uncovering and releasing layer after layer of, fear, judgment, shame and guilt.

(All these negative beliefs are represented as eMaEo, pronounced 'me.' eMaEo stands for 'easing More and *Everything* out'. It is the part of our mind that does not want us to succeed at anything).

This might sound like we have to now live our life, from now on, with a crow bar and dynamite, prying and blasting away each of these layers we've acquired from early childhood (and before). However, this is not the case. In A Course in Miracles it states *"there is no order of difficulty in Miracles"* meaning that, in reality, each layer is equal to all layers.

With a little willingness we begin to realize that these layers *'want' to leave us*. and it is us that are holding onto them. We begin to discover places within us thoughts and beliefs that cause us to turn away from the good things that are trying to come to you in life at a rapid pace and in abundance.

Each layer protects us from our fear of abandonment but they *'also protect us'* from too much success and happiness coming at us all at once with too much intensity.

We discover that, just beneath each layer, a gift of love and abundance awaits us which is greater than the last gift we gained access to and all we have to do is 'let go' in order to have it.

It might sound like there is an infinite number of layers but there are only a few. As our capacity to receive Abundance and Love grows the layers become less and less significant and are let go of faster and easier.

The Most Important Decision You Will Make

Near our deepest self we come upon a question that we must answer, for ourselves, once and for all. Once decided in earnest, either way, we change. Our life will be radically, from then on, different depending upon what we decide.

The Question is... 'at the core of man is he innocent or evil?'

The Case for Evil is Loud and Overwhelming

Overwhelmingly we are confronted with evidence that man is evil. Study history and it seems we have been fighting and killing each other forever with no evidence of it stopping any time soon.

Closer to home... some of us had terrible things happen in our youth. Parents and people who were supposed to love and protect us instead did any number of insane, horrible and, yes some things that looked and felt like 'evil.'

Large prominent religions tell us that we are sinners, we always have been sinners and always will be. Only a few of the thousands of faiths tell us that we are worthy to sit beside god instead of kneeling with our face firmly planted firmly on the floor.

Many cultures worship evil through movies and televisions. Many shows on TV make many things evil... Capitalism, Communism, Globalization., Governments get to choose which countries are evil and which ones are not. And of course, in recent years there is a terrorist or a child molester behind every tree. No one is not to be trusted else they will rob, rape or murder you either in the mall parking lot at night or in your bed while you sleep. Even Alcoholics Anonymous tells us, no matter how much psychological, emotional and spiritual growth we have done *'we are still a drunk but without a drink'* in any given moment.

The Case For Innocence Speaks Softly

All of this evidence of evil can distort our vision and mind so much that Evil is all we can see. It takes a conscious effort to demand our mind to see and feel Innocence. Innocence is much quieter and less obtrusive. It doesn't demand that we see it, rather it invites us to experience Innocence, every day, through small things... a kind word, a smile, a hand across the street. This is the evidence of Innocence. It is there, firmly anchored at our core but often overshadowed by the convincing stories of Evil.

The Choice

Why is this choice so fundamental and absolutely necessary?

Choosing Evil

After due consideration, if we decide Evil is at the core of man then it is perfectly logical for us to be afraid. It is completely understandable and justified to employ, by any means necessary, to protect ourselves and all who we care about from everyone else. Most importantly it is our responsibility to erect ever thickening walls both external and within ourselves to assure that Evil does not reach our core and destroy us before they destroy us.

Choosing Innocence

If on the other hand we choose to believe that man is totally innocent at his core then the walls we build around and inside us are unnecessary barrier that stop us from us experiencing our total Innocence.

"If the walls I have held on to are barriers to experiencing my innate value and innocence then it is my responsibility to do whatever necessary to deconstruct these walls as quickly and as compassionately as I can. The more walls dissolve the more of my loved ones and fellow human being's innocence I will see experience and trust. The more I heal this core belief that the world of man is evil the more layers that I created to protect myself will be lifted from me.

There Is No 'Maybe '

This is the fundamental choice you must decide. It is the responsibility of every human being to choose sooner rather than later. There is no fudging or faking. You can run but you can't hide. This decision determines how you conduct yourself and how you treat every other living thing and the planet they live on. It determines your construct of reality and therefore everything you believe about yourself and others.

There is no choosing just a little bit of evil. Any thought of evil means that man is not 'totally innocent' and therefore any and all barriers to receiving and experiencing love and connection cannot be removed.

A Deeper Connection

Every journey deeper into myself removes barriers to love and innocence. We see for the first time, the systems and strategies we are holding onto are limiting our ability to receive love, innocence and connection. As more layers are dissolved we begin to experience a much deep connection to our 'true self'. We experience that we have a deep connection to the earth, everyone who lives on it. We suddenly realize what we have been thirsty for all along.

Connection and Fulfillment

At our deepest core every human being wants the same things, namely to be really seen, heard, connected to their higher self, and valued without condition. We also have an innate desire to be able to connect with and be received by others.

A lot of the pain that we experience as humans is the pain bouncing back into us from the virtual walls we've erected to protect ourselves from outside hurts, but as Kenny Loggins sings in The Art of Letting Go: *"the gates of hell that you shake 'n you rattle are secretly locked from inside."*

The ability to connect is vital to your success and happiness because the ability to connect to money, good jobs and relationships and to Love are all the same.

If you have something in your life that you have wanted for a long time but still haven't been able to create, acquire, manifest it then at some level it can only be that you are not willing or able to stay connected to it long enough to receive the benefits of having that which you desire. Something inside you is working harder and smarter at stopping you from having it than you are at having it.

Worthiness Is The Gatekeeper

Every moment of every day of our life, no matter how it appears to us, is spent in the pursuit of Connection and Fulfillment. You might take issue with that statement until you've upped your physical, intellectual and emotions capabilities:

> PQ - Physical Intelligence. the ability to care for and maintaining our physical needs for as long as possible.
>
> IQ - Intelligence Quotient, the ability to comprehend and/or understand a combination of reasoning, memory, imagination, and judgment in relation to things used in the real world.
>
> EQ - Emotional Intelligence, the ability to identify, assess, and control our emotions as they relate to ourselves and others.

We used whatever physical strength we have to get out of bed, forage for food. Very quickly after we've fulfilled our basic needs in a way where we know the supply is reliably predictable we begin the pursuit of intelligence to tell us how to understand what we see happening and give us an advantage over our environment so that foraging for food becomes more predictable and we can begin to accumulate things beyond just survival.

Now, if having some strength and some smarts was enough to have the connection and fulfillment we desire we'd likely quit there and enjoy the fruits of our labor. We all have been exposed in some way to the muscular power lifter that spends most of his life in the gym. And we've all been exposed to the Mensa level professor or brilliant engineer who is dumb as a bag of hammers the minute you take them out of their specialty. PQ Intelligence is working with things and making them work for us.

The minute you meet a teacher, a co-worker or a leader of a successful enterprise you realize what the next requirement is for Success... mastery over your emotions and emotional life and being comfortable with others' emotions, no matter what they are.

We quickly learn that PQ and IQ are necessary but not sufficient to be successful because Success involves people and people are emotional beings. Developing and combining PQ and IQ with EQ are the basic ingredients for Achievement and Success.

Intelligence in the 21st Century

Just being aware of, and to a degree in control of, our emotions, is no longer enough to maximize our potential. To the first three quotients I would add another three:

> **CQ** – The understanding and awareness of the different constructs of reality of people in their social and cultural environments around the world. Another way to say this is to be able to relate to everyone no matter what 'tribe' they are from.
>
> **SQ** – Spiritual Intelligence, our ability to connect with the God that we envision in our minds.
>
> *(SQ can be explained as our ability to connect holistically, to recognize synchronicity and the energy that flows in and through all things. SQ is our ability to allow things to be true without proof.)*
>
> **WQ** – Worthiness Quotient is our ability to attract, receive and allow ourselves to have all the benefits of everything that brings us fulfillment.

Within our worthiness quotient is our ability to connect with all things seen and unseen, known and unknown and to allow ourselves to have a compassionate relationship with them all. It is our ability to function without judgment on ourselves and others. It is our ability to connect with and allow ourselves to receive everything we want to have and achieve. And, our worthiness quotient is our ability to allow all good things to come to us all the time, all at once and in abundance without becoming fearful or overwhelmed.

One of the difficulties with understanding and utilizing our worthiness quotient to assist in creating our best life possible is that WQ cannot be measured. There is no test that will determine your WQ. You will only know what it was overall at the end of your life if you do a life review and make an assessment of what you connected to and achieved versus what your vision of your life was at an early age.

"Your life is what you make it." Understanding your Worthiness Quotient is a key ingredient in making your life everything you envision it can be and even more.

Connectedness - Our Deepest Desire

All Humans have the capacity to feel connected to each other and to everything in the Universe, all at the same time. While that is so, it is not the subject of this book. Almost all of us have had an experience, even if for only half a second, that we are connected to something greater than ourselves.

On January 31, 1971, Navy Captain Dr. Edgar Mitchell embarked on a journey into outer space that resulted in his becoming the sixth man to walk on the moon. The Apollo 14 mission was NASA's third manned lunar landing.

Travelling back to Earth, having just walked on the moon, Dr. Mitchell, a trained engineer and scientist, had what is known as a spontaneous Santori experience. He left NASA and has spent the rest of his life in pursuit of an understanding of Connectedness.

A Santori is a profound experience of 'Oneness' for an extended period of time where we know that we are all connected to each other and everything in a very real way. Have an undeniable experience of true Connectedness just once and you will spend the rest of your life learning how to live in Connectedness all the time. It is not that rare. Many thousands of people alive today have had the experience. Success takes on a whole new meaning after that.

This book is not about Spirituality. It is about realizing and experiencing your true Worthiness, which is to realize that we are infinitely valuable and totally innocent. A momentary glimpse of this reality gives us a knowing at our core that we are worthy today, that we have always been, and that we always will. This is a non-negotiable fact that we are and will be no matter what we say or have said, do or have done, experience or have experienced and observe or have observed.

How close have you come to this knowingness? Probably a million miles or two. Every day living in this world, for the most part, provides us with continuous and ample evidence that we are anything but Worthy.

Before you go blaming your parents, the media, the government or those idiot drivers that share the commute with you every day, think about how you are also a co-conspirator in manifesting both societal and your own personal unworthiness.

Probably very little in your daily life is going to push you in the right direction, so your current level of worthiness, which I call your 'Worthiness Quotient' (WQ), is going to remain pretty much the same as it is now or get worse. If you are okay with that, then great. Far be it for anyone to try and change your mind, but if you're not satisfied with your level of 'receiving all that life has to offer' then you've made a good investment in this book.

> "May you realize sooner rather than later that you are the person your dog knows you are"

I surmise that more people have their first experiences of Connection not with people but with their pets. People lie; their motivations are unclear and their own blocks to Connection make it often difficult for anyone to be clear enough to feel and maintain the connection. So the first one to be grateful to is your animal friends.

Fulfillment of Our Dreams, Desires and Purpose

The other deep desire we have is for Fulfillment, (a combination of achievement, balance and integrity). We are all meaning-making machines. By the end of our life we hope we've achieved fulfillment in every area of our life. Often times our idea of fulfillment is not really 'our' idea. Our parents, families, educators, employers, spouses and society itself all have ideas of what our definition of Fulfillment should be.

> **What do you Love?**
> **What do you do well?**
> **What will the world pay you for?**
> **What does the world need?**
> **What does my soul want to learn?**

The overlap of these four circles is what gives you Satisfaction, Comfort, Bliss, Contentment and Fulfillment.

Ask yourself these questions, and write down the answers. Keep them where you can refer to them often. With all the push-me/pull-me going on in the world and all the forces that have an agenda we can easily lose sight of what Fulfillment means to us?

Worthiness is By Nature Holistic

Understanding Worthiness requires you to first acquire what I call 3D thinking, which is something that doesn't come easily to most of us, at least not at this time in our development.

Most people can, with a few minutes of training and practice, juggle two apples in the air. The jump from two apples to three however (just one more apple), is a different proposition altogether.

A high percentage of people (over 50 percent), cannot remember all 10 digits of a typical phone number within one minute of having had them read to them. In that moment you also ask them about a painful experience they had in the past and the number of those unable to recall rises to 80 percent.

Here's the challenge that gets in the way of us experiencing our own innate worth... we think about 60,000 thoughts a day and 95 percent are the same thoughts and questions we asked yesterday. We are asking ourselves questions about the past every minute of every day, only a small percentage of which we are conscious of asking.

Worthiness is so up close and personal. It comes from much deeper parts of our mind. With all these unruly thoughts making so much noise our Worthiness for the most part is invisible. How to benefit from what it tells us is almost completely outside of our everyday awareness. Being so close to us we've hardly ever experienced its power, so can't even conceptualize what it is and how it works. It's is like the little fish saying to the big fish: *"What the hell is this ocean you keep talking about?"*

Like the wind, we don't experience Worthiness itself but experience the results of a low worthiness quotient. We seldom employ Worthiness principles at times we need them most. We have no practice at using our Worthiness to interrupt old habits and patterns, which results in us *"being at the train station when our ship comes in."*

Hiding From Happiness

As human beings we are clever, very clever... often too clever for our own good! We learn how to successfully hide from ourselves. Over time we accumulate judgments, beliefs and suspicions about ourselves... all evidence that we are not as good a person as we project out onto the world. Dr. Chuck Spezzano calls this: *"locking yourself IN the cage WITH the gorilla."*

You Can't Hide Half A Thought!

Our *'cleverality'* allows us, very successfully, to hide most of these judgments and beliefs from ourselves. We spend huge amounts of energy keeping them from bubbling to the surface. We end up being at the mercy of these thoughts even though we don't remember really where we got them or what they are.

You can't bury half a thought so you also end up burying the thoughts that would lead to solutions and prosperity. We do come up with answers and solutions but these are also the effect of this layer of judgments and often don't have the intended result.

Actually that is not really accurate. The solutions we arrive at always have exactly the intended result. They match our Worthiness Quotient perfectly. We always get what we intend ourselves to have.

> *"We can spend our whole lives escaping
> from the monsters of our minds"*
>
> ~Pema Chödrön, from 'When Things Fall Apart'

Worthiness – A Universal Phenomena

Is your life what you thought it was going to be? If it isn't then the difference between what you thought it would be and what it now is, almost certainly has something to do with Worthiness.

What Gets In Our Way?

The challenge of our construct of reality is that it is largely two dimensional. It seems to us that most of the time we only have two choices and this sets up conflicts within our mind that run constantly and stop us from having a direct path to 'enlightenment.'

Living Immersed in Conflicting Needs

As human beings we operate, moment by moment within a sea of Polarities within a construct of reality known as Duality.

Our Basic Needs

Tony Robbins lists, in his Unleash 'The Power Within', (Robbins) believes we have five human needs. To me these represent the things 'we think' we need for us to be fulfilled.

> *Certainty/Comfort* - We all want comfort. And much of this comfort comes from certainty.
>
> *Variety* - At the same time as we want certainty, we also crave variety.
>
> *Significance* - We want our life to have meaning and significance. Connection/Love. We want to be cared for and cared about. We want to become better, to improve to stretch.
>
> *Contribution* - We want to contribute something of value, to help others, to make the world a better place.

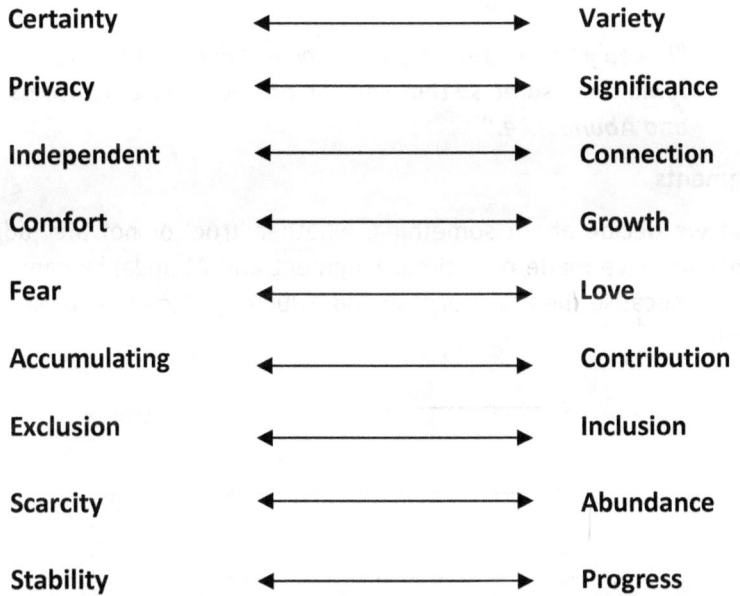

Certainty	**Variety**
Privacy	**Significance**
Independent	**Connection**
Comfort	**Growth**
Fear	**Love**
Accumulating	**Contribution**
Exclusion	**Inclusion**
Scarcity	**Abundance**
Stability	**Progress**

They also show us the need related conflicts that constantly fluctuate and cause confusion, frustration and lack of progress. Any 'lack' we are experiencing is caused by at least two conflicting needs being equally as strong.

NEEDS. *(Never Ending Emotional Demands)* are all fueled by one thing. *'Fear'*. Dr. Chuck Spezzano wrote a book called 'If It Hurts It Isn't Love'" In the introduction Spezzano *states "if it hurts it isn't Love because Love by its very nature does not hurt."*

So, if Love doesn't hurt then what does hurt? 'Needs' hurt. Hollywood and many country and western songs tell us so.

Fundamentally we need people and we need them to do things for us. This makes us vulnerable and not in control. In order to mitigate this vulnerability we put pressure on others to make us feel more safe. It is always about the other person, the external world.

"I need you to be a certain way for me to be happy"

"I need you because a part of me is missing and I need you to make me whole."

"I need my friend to apologize because I'm right and she is wrong."

"I need the world to be a certain way or how I view the world must be wrong. Everyone will find out and I will be abandoned."

The Need that does the most damage is also one of the more difficult to understand.

> *"I need you, my partner, sister, boss, addict, society to remain the same so that you can protect me from Success and Abundance."*

Judgments

What we decide about something, whether 'true' or not are judgments we have made over time. Judgment and Abundance cannot co-exist because the only purpose and value of judgment is to keep us safe.

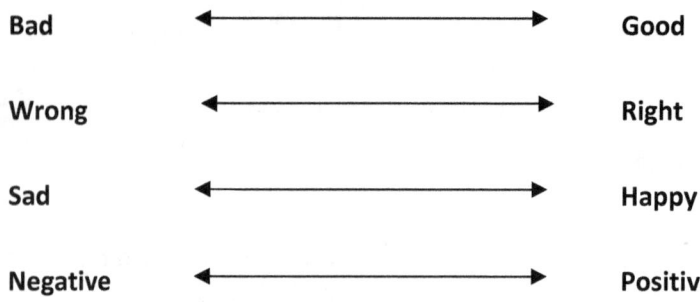

"Judgments are decisions that produce thoughts, feelings, emotions that always cause us to turn towards that which we believe is safe."

Polarizations

Polarizations are an outgrowth of our individual needs and judgments that evolves into groups of people taking a stand on something and other people taking the opposite view of how things work and how to make them better. Often a group's stance becomes more extreme than their actual, privately held beliefs.

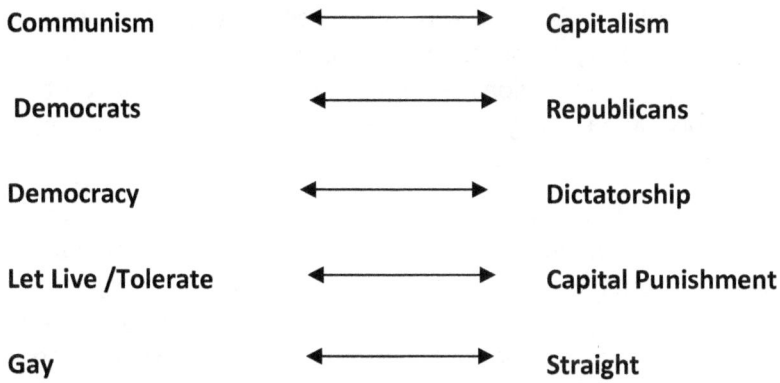

Communism	←——→	**Capitalism**
Democrats	←——→	**Republicans**
Democracy	←——→	**Dictatorship**
Let Live /Tolerate	←——→	**Capital Punishment**
Gay	←——→	**Straight**

Polarizations are often considered and shows as left / right along a spectrum. The Tea party is considered to be to the right of the Republican party which is considered right of the Democratic Party.

Duality

> "Out beyond ideas of wrongdoing and rightdoing there is a field. I'll meet you there."
>
> ~ Rumi

Duality And Our Constructs Of Reality

(From Wikipedia, the free encyclopedia) Dualism can mean the tendency of humans to perceive and understand the world as being divided into two overarching categories. In this sense, it is dualistic when one perceives a tree as a thing separate from everything surrounding it, or when one perceives a "self" that is distinct from the rest of the world. In traditions such as classical Hinduism, Zen Buddhism or Islamic Sufism, a key to enlightenment is "transcending" this sort of dualistic thinking, without merely substituting dualism

with monism or pluralism. By combining modern day quantum physics with early Buddhism duality is considered to be states of consciousness and that the only things that exist are momentary quantum particles, much like quarks, electrons, etc. (Dualism)

All personal and spiritual growth requires us to first understand our selves as we have come to be. First we have all the combinations of ups and downs in our body systems and brain. In our mind we experience emotions and feelings moment by moment resulting in drives, wants, desires, needs and judgments.

Because we live in a world with other people who have different needs, beliefs and judgments we are pulled back and forth along the spectrum from polarizations on issues that we believe are important to our survival and progress as a society. All of these factors combine to become what is known as our 'construct of reality.'

Our construct of reality is how we believe things work in our world. We believe that when you drop something it falls to the ground. We believe we can't walk through walls or live without oxygen. We 'know' from observing how the world works that there are certain common ways to survive and rise in our society towards those things that are good.

It is believed that man has been on the earth in our current form for about 110,000 years. Overall the choices mankind have made must have been more appropriate than not or we wouldn't be here. We wouldn't have survived. Some believe that today, our current construct of reality has been so similar for so long that it is actually carried forward in our DNA.

The Need For A Single Theme and Pattern

Living day by day we can't remain actively conscious, nor take the time necessary to consider all the factors of why we do the things we do in order to survive and prosper. There is too much data. We would surely go nuts and if we didn't we would certainly become more and more ineffective in our pursuit of happiness, connection and fulfillment.

To function and gain awareness of what is going on in and around us we need to combine all this data into a Theme that explains our motivations and location along the path to our ultimate destination and rewards.

The more perspective we gain as to how 'we' seek and where we've decided we will find fulfillment, the more we will understand Worthiness and how it factors in.

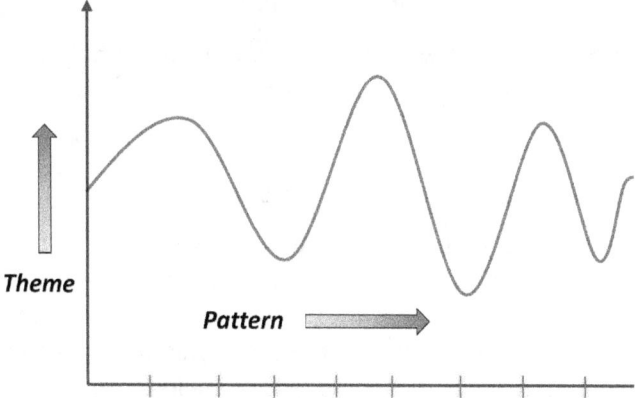

All of these motivations and methods of getting to where we want to go can be summed up in four basic ways of thinking. Within these four themes we believe we will get our needs met and progressing in the world throughout life. We ultimately seek happiness and fulfillment within what I call 'the four quadrants of fulfillment.'

> *"The more original a discovery, the more obvious it seems afterwards."*
>
> ~ Arthur Koestler

The Four Quadrants Of Fulfillment

All these combinations of body and mind ultimately form our thoughts, emotions and feelings that combine to become our attitudes, beliefs, stance and states of being.

These four fundamental ways of being are what we believe will result in us getting our needs met and make progress in the world throughout our life.

Our Outer Journey - Quadrants One & Two

(More is More) The first two quadrants provide us with an holistic experience of life through the world that exists outside ourselves. The outside world exists whether we are in it or not. It was here before we arrived and it will be here long after we are gone. This outer world is largely experienced by everyone in the same way. It is what others see when they look at us and see how we do our life. It is what we do, how we operate, what strategies we employ to achieve, what we accumulate and how we justify it. It contains all our thoughts, beliefs and judgments that come under the category of 'More is More.' The focus of this part of our mind is on 'I'.

All motivations and strategies for accomplishment in our outer world can be divided up into two main groups:

Going Out And Getting

In today's world our pursuit of Fame, Wealth, and Success has never been more intense. We 'go for it' in every possible way. Most of us play by the rules but going out and 'taking and grabbing' are not so rare. You can probably think back to a time when you grabbed something you had a need for.

Going Out And Giving

Going out and giving, is where we switch our focus onto 'others'. We care about all kinds of things - animals, minorities, the environment and every other thing in the world that needs assistance to be able to live a better life.

> *"Everyone is running from something. But if we're lucky, really lucky, fate intervenes and presents an opportunity to conquer our fears. Only then, if triumphant, can a destiny bestowed become a destiny fulfilled."*
>
> ~ Rome Sims

The Four Quadrants Of Fulfillme

Our Inner Journey *(LESS is More)*

Going Within and Allowing		Going Withii Receivin
(Passive)		(Pro-activ

Our Outer Journey *(MORE is More)*

Going Out and Giving		Going Out ar Getting
(Giving to Have)		(Going Out and Tak

Our Inner Journey - Quadrants Three & Four

(Less is More) The first two of the four quadrants of the mind are focused on the external. The remaining two are focused on our inner world. Our inner world is completely unique to us. It exists only because we experience it. It was fresh to the world when we arrived and it will go with us when we cease to exist in the outer world. Our inner world also has two quadrants and therefore two different themes:

Going Within and Allowing

Our spiritual life has many aspects. One is our strategy for accessing an understanding of Connection. We fall silent and allow any and all thoughts to rise without judgment. By removing as much of the meaning we attached to thoughts and memories we are able to clear our mind of meaningless chatter and have a deeper experience of our inner world and connection.

Remaining Within and Receiving

Receiving is the fourth quadrant of our holistic mind. Receiving is not attracting. It is what we do after our going out and getting and our attracting has been successful. Receiving is allowing to take into ourselves the value of things coming at us faster than we are normally used to. Receiving is part of our Inner journey. It is often viewed as 'passive' but it is anything but. Upping your Worthiness Quotient it is a very pro-active, choice-driven act.

A sudden lotto winner is not accustomed to money coming at them in such quantity, as quickly as it did and with such little effort. We' re quickly overwhelmed and meltdown when our ability to receive is bombarded.

What Do We Know About Receiving?

Of the Four Quadrants of Fulfillment, Receiving is the one we know the least about. Our society and culture concentrates all of its education and efforts on 'going out and getting', to the exclusion of allowing ourselves to have the benefits of struggle, hard work, intelligence and good fortune. Receiving is also our ability to allow in good luck and what came to us for no good reason that we know of.

"It is better to give than to receive."

A Google Search on the quote *"it is better to give than to receive"* yields over 27 million pages.

(For all you contrarians out there a search on *"It is better to receive than to give"* yields 16,800 and many of those were in the form of a question 'when is it better to receive than to give?).

Searching on *"learn to receive"* yields 162,000 or so, which is 5.8 percent of the idea that giving is better. Now, either we have learned all about Receiving or the idea of being worthy to receive is not a conversation we are having yet.

The Four Quadrants Combined

The Four Quadrants combined is where our quest for connection and fulfillment is played out. The Worthiness Cycle brings all quadrants to together into something we can grasp and impact.

Worthiness is our ability to know and experience our innate value and divine innocence. The Worthiness Cycle bring all the elements into one Cycle where we can see where and how we are moving us toward, or away, from Connection and Fulfillment.

Definitions of a Cycle

There are two definitions of a Cycle help us to understand more of how the Worthiness Cycle works:

9. A periodically repeated sequence of events
10. A continuous change or a sequence of changes in the state of a system that leads to the restoration of the system to its original state after a finite period of time

Most cycles have a unit of measurement that represents a real number: i.e. the price of a particular stock on the stock market, over the last year. The cycle is not a measurement of the details of your life. i.e. how many arguments you had with your spouse or how many days last month that you meditated, the number of 'down' days or 'up' days.

Think of the Worthiness Cycle as a meshing of Themes, Patterns and States of Mind

Two terms describe momentum you have up and down: Heading for heaven like a homesick angel, and Hell bent on destruction.

Dianetics has a term they call 'clear' which helps us in understanding the Worthiness Cycle.

(I've modified their description to remove some of the terms unique to Scientology: http://en.wikipedia.org/wiki/Clear_(Scientology))

"Clear" in Dianetics is a level a person can achieve on the way to their personal salvation. A state of Clear is reached when a person becomes free of the influence of memory, trances consisting of unwanted emotions or painful traumas not readily available to the conscious mind.

Dianetics says that human beings accumulate anxieties, psychosomatic illnesses, and aberrations due to experiencing 'memory trances' throughout their lives. Unlike the concept of Enlightenment every single person can reach Clear with some training.

> **Aberration:** *a departure from rational thought or behavior, i.e. to err, to make mistakes, or more specifically to have fixed ideas which are not true.*

A person is said to be a Clear when s/he *"no longer has their own 'reactive mind'* and therefore suffers none of the ill effects that the reactive mind can cause." A Clear is said to be "at cause over" (in control of) their "mental energy" (their thoughts), and able to think clearly (Observer) even when faced with the very situation that in earlier times caused them difficulty.

Your Unique Worthiness Cycle

Only you can say where you are in the Worthiness Cycle at any given time. Others familiar with the Worthiness Cycle can get an idea from the words you use to describe what's going on for you at a particular time but only you know how often you are *'clear.'*

Direction Indicators

You are heading up or about to head up when:

- you feel light as in mood and attitude.
- your life feels lighter than it has been as it is 'in the flow.'
- you are in your observer/participant where you are aware of your thoughts and behaviors and have the presence of mind to intervene when necessary.
- you feel inspired. - you feel like you are on purpose - you are 'in integrity.' - have your basic needs met with some surplus (Abundant).
- you are in a state of elation: do not feel in reaction about anything in particular.
- you have good things coming to you that are 'miracles' because you have no clear understanding of "why me, why now?"
- you are in a state of anxiety caused from being uncomfortable because you are receiving too much Abundance too quickly, not giving you an opportunity to 'catch your breath'.

You are heading down, or at the point of changing direction downward when:

- you are in a state of anger or fear.
- you feel you have lost control of events.
- you are in a state of agitation, depression, despair, lethargy.
- you are reacting to a person, place or thing.
- you do not have all that you need to sustain your life.
- you are saying, doing things that not in integrity.
- you are feeling heavy, like life is 'dragging you down'.
- you are immersed in a chronic illness.
- you lost control to thoughts of rejection, revenge, control.
- you are under the control of habits and addictions.

The Space Between Your Thoughts

Music is both the notes and the spaces between the notes. If there are no spaces there is no recognizable music. The symphony is the space between the notes and those between the individual instruments.

Deepak Chopra speaks about expanding the length of silence between thoughts. Expanding the length of time allows you to process what the thought actually is and where it's going to take you if you follow it, and it allows you to add thoughts that support the first thought.

Get good at this and you can literally watch a thought form in your mind, watch it come towards you, experience it entering into you and then exiting and then you watch it leave and dissipate.

The more expanded the time, the more time you have to evoke your inner Observer/Participant and not react to that thought, which if allowed to draw up other thoughts in that particular neronetwork, will head you in a 'death' direction rather than a 'life' direction.

You can do this. Quantum Physics shows that every atom in your body is 99% space so the ability to allow space is built into your DNA.

Worthiness Cycle Timeframes

We go through the Worthiness Cycle hourly, daily, weekly, monthly etc. Often we hear that someone was in a 'seven-year cycle' and a ten-year cycle and a lifelong cycle.

We go through the cycle second by second. Gaining space between the thoughts is the only real way to identify, and have an effect on, which direction that thought points us towards.

With this in mind we can say that we have several Worthiness Cycles, of different lengths, intersecting with each other. The Worthiness Cycle we display in this book is a single cycle made up of all the cycles outlined above.

Learn Your Trigger Points

A *'trigger point'* is an event in time, (it could be two to three seconds), that causes us to stop and change direction. It goes by so quickly we hardly know it's there.

(I was in a relationship for almost five years where, for example, we would be almost out the door on our way to a picnic on a beautiful sunny day. We both wanted to go to the picnic and to be with each other. One of us would say something 'off the cuff' that had no particular meaning and the other person would say something and within 45 seconds we would be in the fight of our lives.

The odd thing was that it was never about something that had been building, like a grievance that had been allowed to fester. One minute we were in heaven in our minds and the next we'd be in hell that would have one of us, (usually me), walking out the door and neither of us talking to each other for a week or two. It happened dozens of times and we never got ahead of the trigger points for the entire five years we were together.)

The Truth is Always Positive

The worthiness cycle is always showing us the current trend. With fresh awareness and training we learn to interrupt a negative trend once it has caused us to change direction and start heading away from 'our truth.' Your objective is to be able to interrupt that trigger 'before' we change direction and head down towards

You can get a good sense of where you are in the cycle at any point, If you zoom back out as if you were recording with a video camera and 'de-focus' on the details. What has the trend been over the last, day, week, year?

All Worthiness is in the 'Now'

The first and most important step is to notice that something has changed. What you are paying attention to is your feelings. Something feels different. It doesn't have to be someone punching or yelling at us or something that we really don't like. Anything can be a trigger that sets off a reaction resulting in us changing direction"

- Some smell has drifted our way.
- Someone has a particular look on their face.
- Someone has said something, maybe just one word.
- Some sound no matter how low the volume has happened.
- Someone has entered the room, (or the building) we are in or close to.
- Something, our intuition is telling us, is about to happen or has just happened.

What ever it is and there can be hundreds of them a day it has caused our feelings to be affected. Most of these triggers are so slight they go by. We have to get in tune with our feelings in a deep meaningful way. We don't necessarily have to know what the event was and we don't need to know why that event happened. What we need to be aware of is that something has happened and we have reacted.

From Reaction to Observation

Here is a process for to aid you in improving your worthiness response: Immediately, as soon as you sense something has changed ask yourself the following:

- Something has happened and I feel different than I did a minute, hour, week, month, year ago.
- What am I feeling right now and what I am feeling under that feeling?
- Am I triggered?
- Am I triggered enough to stop me on my journey to success, happiness and fulfillment?
- When exactly was I triggered?
- What situation and/or past perception caused me to be triggered now?
- What have been the consequences so far?
- How often have I had negative consequences from this or something similar?
- What Is Really Happening Here Now?
- What do I need to move back into the center of myself?
- Do I, in this moment, have access to the physical, mental and Psycho/Spiritual, (internal) resources necessary to interrupt this pattern successfully or do I need to access someone in the external?
- What will the consequences be of moving back into the Vision I have dedicated myself to?

The idea is to learn how to realize that you have turned away from Abundance and to intercede to get turned back to be heading in an up direction. Without a process for recognizing and acting in a proactive way it could be hours, months and maybe even years before you realized you're now heading in the wrong direction. The goal is to know yourself so well and be 'in the now' so clearly that you catch yourself in mid-thought and never do change direction. It will take a while I can assure you.

Your Worthiness Cycle Step By Step

First Step: Learn To Be The Observer On Demand

You as the Observer

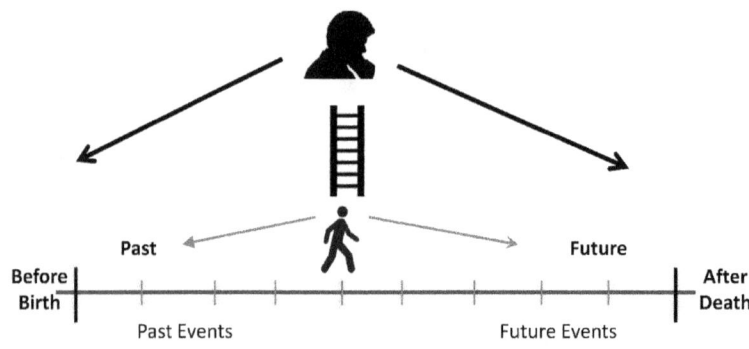

Your Life Events Timeline

All humans have an innate ability to rise above their life and become 'The Observer' of the events past, present and future. This has been written about for centuries. Much can be found on the internet about how to put this into practice.

Not only can we learn to become The Observer but we are able to be both the Observer and the *'active'* Participant at the same time.

Not only can we *'see'* from the Observer point of view what is happening, has happened and what is going to happen, you as the Observer, from the Observer's point of view, can *'experience'* what you as the Participant are experiencing as well.

Being the Observer / Participant allows us to see much more clearly what happened in the past and much more of what is going to happen in the future.

This is the only way to gain a better grasp on what really happened in the past, not how we remember/perceive it. We then can see what is actually us taking our past and 'projecting it onto the future.'

We all project our past onto the future. You are doing it every day and therefore your future is going to be more like the past than you probably want, unless you learn how to be the Observer AND the Participant much of the time.

One of the most challenging things to remember is to move to Observer/Participant when we need to most, in conflicts with others and when we have let our 'I need to be right' about something get out of control. This timeline might end when we die but if it doesn't we gain a much larger and broader perspective if we view our life as being a thousand years long.

Sometimes the only way things make sense is to look at it from a 'spiritual' perspective. Life is really quite uninteresting if we only view our life as flat. The second dimension of our life is how high will we rise into life with a second dimension. On the Vertical axis we measure what we all want in life.

Life's Ups and Downs

The Worthiness Cycle shows us the roller coaster ride we experience in life in relation to the four quadrants of fulfillment... what we think we want or need to gain happiness and fulfillment. It shows how our needs, drives and rewards play out in everyday life. You've probably heard the saying 'life has its ups and downs." Your Worthiness Cycle explains what those ups and downs actually are and why we experience life in this way.

Our Life's Time Line

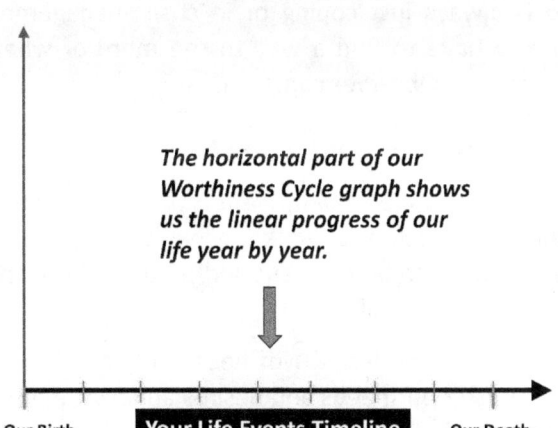

We begin by looking at our life line early along a single line. (an idea as a result of (Information on Timeline Theory)

http://www.nlpcoaching.com/what-is-time-line-therapy.html

This is the timeline of our lives. Somewhere on the line is where you are right now. Everything behind this point is your past. Everything ahead of this point is your future.

As we organize time in this way, we tend to flash pictures along the line from left to right. This helps us to know what happened first, what happened second etc. It teaches us cause and effect. We can see how things we do create other things. It helps us to see what we need to do next in order to accomplish the things we want to in life. It helps us see that there is space between the events in our life and therefore there are spaces between our thoughts.

Most people visualize their past behind them in their mind and their future in front of them. This is why we say, *"we're leaving the past and walking into the future."*

(Ask yourself where you have stored your memories. Some people discover that they talk about the events of the past as if they were today. They discover that they have stored their past ahead instead of behind. Change is a lot more difficult if we are "walking into our past instead of our future.")

The only challenge with standing rooted on the line, trying to see and understand your future, is that the pictures tend to pile up one in front of the other. We can't see beyond the first few pictures. You can't see much of what's going to happen in the more distant future. Our natural born intuition isn't able to do its work for you. Are you a person who is always just coping or in crisis management most of the time? You have to find a way to see more of what's going on. This is where your Observer comes in.

We want Abundance and we want it now!

We all want money, but what we actually want is more money than we need plus a little bit more so that we know we will survive. We also want the flow of money to be constant and predictable so that we will be safe in the future as well.

Abundance is what we actually desire. Not necessarily a lot at any one time but enough to suit our needs and desires and a little more. This holds true for everything. We want food, shelter, friends. We want more than we need plus a little bit more.

Total Abundance of everything we can dream of plus more we can call <u>Everything</u> and <u>Nothing</u> is the total Absence of Abundance.

Abundance of Everything

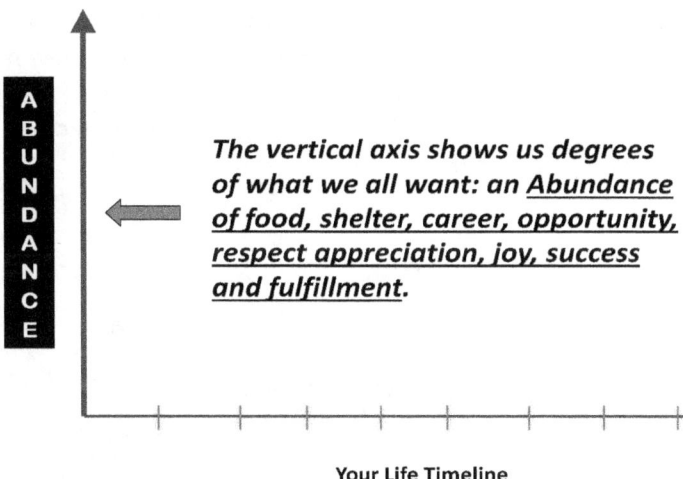

The vertical axis shows us degrees of what we all want: an <u>Abundance of food, shelter, career, opportunity, respect appreciation, joy, success and fulfillment</u>.

Your Life Timeline

We might still have some things but if they don't serve a need for us then they don't mean anything to us.

The Worthiness Arena

Worthiness encompasses the full Abundance available to us and the entirety of our lives from birth to death. We live out our lives in the Worthiness Zone and are never out of it. This is one of the reasons that Worthiness has escaped our notice up until now.

The Worthiness Zone

Everything

Worthiness encompasses the total Abundance available over our Lifetime.

Nothing

Your Life Timeline

Your Worthiness Setpoint (WSP)

All of us have a degree of life's abundance that we are comfortable with. As a result all of us establish an initial *'Worthiness Setpoint.'* This Setpoint is a reflection of our decision and our world view of how much Abundance is available in the world and how much of it we deserve to have. You set your WSP very early in life, probably within the first month after you are born. Many factors combine and average out to determine where the WSP is set:

Your Worthiness Setpoint

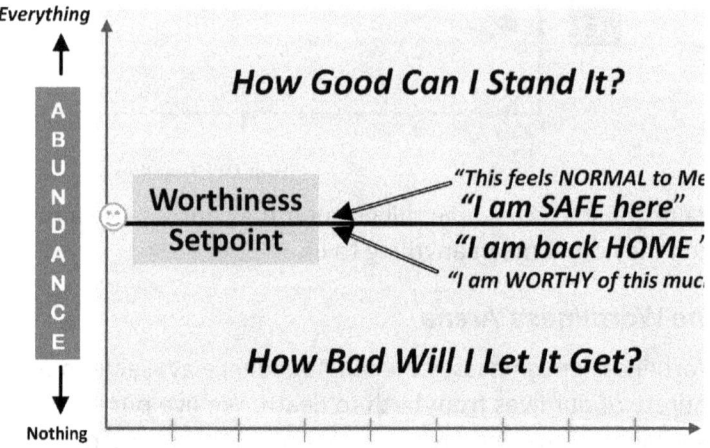

- Your experiences of Abundance and Anxiety in the womb from the moment of conception until your birth. i.e. was there enough nutrition and was it continuous? Were there manmade toxins like alcohol or drugs like cocaine? What about environmental toxins?

- Your birth experience. Was it easy, harsh, noisy, lights too bright? Was there 'panic' in the air?

- Your initial bonding with your mother. Was your mother happy to see you or was she so sick that she wasn't available when you wanted to re-connect with her outside of the womb and bond to assure yourself that you were going to be okay?

- The type and intensity of the energy that was around you in the formative years. Were your parents excited to have you or were you the last they were going to have?

- Were they nervous and afraid? Did you get fed, changed and held as much as you needed to feel safe? Were they unhappy with each other? Were your siblings happy to have you or were they jealous right from start? Was 'conflict' in the air?
- Information in your DNA brought forward from your ancestry. Was there a lot of loss, happiness, abundance in your family tree?
- Adding and combining all the information and how it made you feel you decided what the world is all about. With the mind of an infant you made a judgment call as to how much Abundance there is in the world. You decided how much was available to you and how much crying and struggle you were going to do to get it.

Our Worthiness Setpoint is set so early in life that we don't have a sense of ever living without it and at the level it's at. It will feel natural for it to be at a certain level, and everything better and worse than that original Setpoint is going to produce some kind of anxiety and fear.

How Good Can I Stand It?

Your Worthiness Setpoint is a single point of view that you have chosen. You know that there is more life out there.

In the Worthiness Cycle everything that is above our initial Worthiness Setpoint is a territory *called "How Good Can I Stand It?"* Below our initial WSP the territory is known as *"How Bad Will I Let It Get?"*

In "How Good Can I Stand It?"we are hanging out in 'Above The Worthiness Setpoint Line Thinking.' These thoughts feed actions that lead to Abundance. We are asking ourselves, (mostly subconsciously), how much Abundance can I achieve and receive before I have to stop, turn away from and then run like hell from in fear of things getting too good.

How Bad Will I Let It Get?

In "How Bad Will I Let It Get?" we are in Below The Worthiness Setpoint Line Thinking. These thoughts feed actions that lead to Nothing. Because humans are hard wired to 'rise' towards Everything we sooner or later have to come to the realization that we are choosing to stay on a path to our own destruction and we are choosing at each new 'bottom' that we reach whether we want to live or die.

Self Esteem, Self Worth and Worthiness

Much has been written about Self Esteem and Self Worth. Both of these are states. Although our self-esteem, and self worth do rise and fall throughout our life they do not function the same as Worthiness. Worthiness is a wave that is fluid.

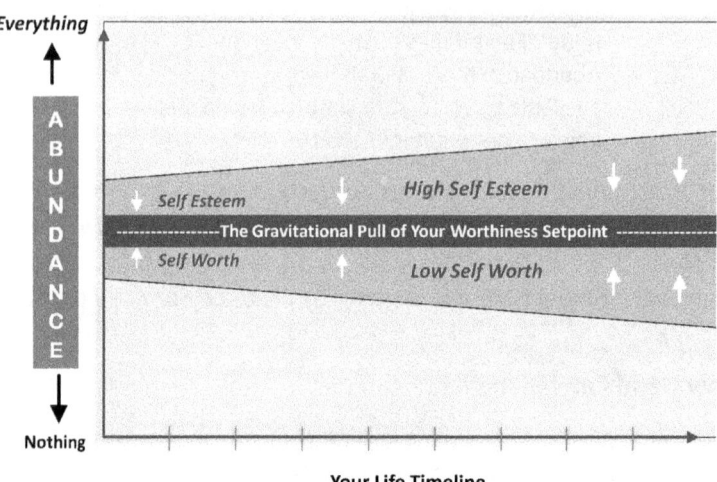

Your Self Esteem and Self Worth

Our definition of Self Esteem is a feeling state. We feel good about ourselves so we say we have self esteem. In order to improve our self esteem we do things, (outside ourselves), that make us feel good. We buy some new clothes or risk a new hair style, which improves how we 'feel' about ourselves therefore raising our self esteem to a new level.

Self Worth is a measurement of how much we feel we are worth, mostly in relation to other people. We learn to communicate better. We expand our education and get a promotion which improves our self worth.

In terms of the Worthiness Cycle you don't really know or understand the concept of self esteem until the first time you rise above your Worthiness Setpoint and/or fall below it for the first time. At this point you identify your self esteem which is just above your Worthiness Setpoint and your self-worth is just below your Worthiness Setpoint.

Self Esteem is just above the WSP because we have no interest in, nor do we create, esteem that is less than we started with. When we talk about self esteem we always say that someone has self esteem or high self esteem.

On the other hand when we talk about self worth we tend to talk about 'low' self worth. Given that initially you have never been below your WSP you would not have experienced 'less than' yet. Self Worth doesn't show up until we enter the *"How Bad Will I Let It Get?"* area.

The Gravitational Pull of Worthiness Setpoint

The minute we move away from our Worthiness Setpoint we feel that something is different. We don't feel quite ourselves and start to evaluate what is happening in order to determine if we are safe and if we are heading somewhere we want to make sure that we are heading in a direction that is good.

This pull is with us our entire life and gets stronger as we move farther and farther away from it.

As both Self Esteem and Self Worth are located very close to your WSP they are very much affected by the draw of the Worthiness Setpoint. The minute we start to do something, that will improve our esteem and/or worth, the gravitation pull of our WSP starts to draw on and retard their expansion.

Viewing Needs, Polarity and Duality Differently

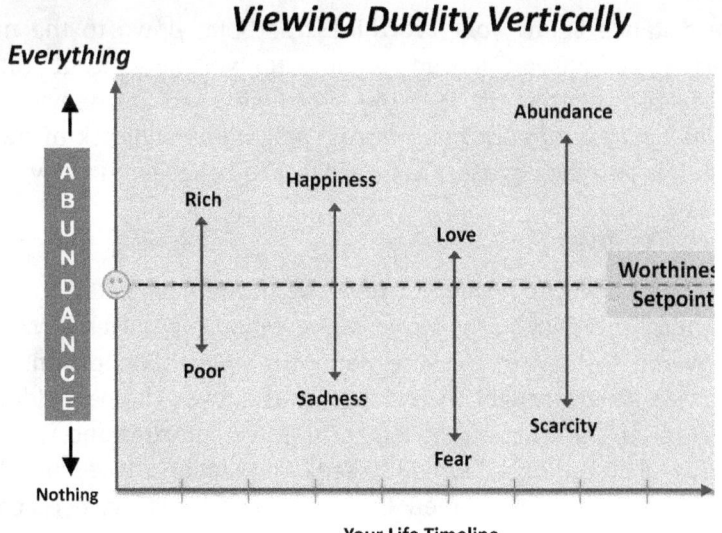

Earlier Needs, Polarities and Duality were presented as something for us to be aware of in our quest to understand Worthiness and how it plays a part in our lives. For some reason we have become accustomed to viewing these things on a horizontal plane from left to right. In the Worthiness Cycle Model we flip them to the vertical.

Viewing them vertically shows why we begin to naturally rise above our worthiness set point. For self preservation we are hard wired to continually rise towards Happiness, Love, Abundance and away from Fear and Scarcity. We are intuitively drawn towards things that will do us the most good.

Viewing Duality differently by moving from left to right thinking to rising and descending thinking we can also understand more easily our growth in some areas and not in others. We might, for example have risen higher in our ability to allow Happiness than we have in our ability to allow ourselves to receive Love. We might have got use to experiencing more Fear than we have Sadness. Growth is not linier nor is it reciprocal. Just because you have learned hw to allow more Abundance doesn't mean that you learned how to allow less scarcity at the same time.

Our Abundance Allowance Range

The distance between how much Happiness we can consistently allow and arriving at 'Everything' represents our potential for growth in that area.

Unrealized' Worthiness

The distance below your Worthiness Setpoint down to the most Scarcity you have allowed is not 'un-worthiness' but rather 'unrealized' worthiness. It is the Worthiness we are denying ourselves because of conflicting needs, judgments and lack of awareness. It is also the degree of your wiliness to believe in Scarcity.

More Receiving (MOR)

As human beings our deepest desire is to feel connected to everyone and everything in the world, some would say Universe. We are hardwired to head in the direction of complete Connection. Mankind has always sought to find out what is over the next ridge. A program in our minds' DNA that I call MOR activates and we intuitively launch out on a journey to seek Connections, Love and Abundance. We are programmed to not stop until we have reached, gathered and received *Everything.*

Heading Up To 'Everything'

The path to Everything is always up from wherever we start so we intuitively begin to rise towards the life force and connection we knew in the womb.

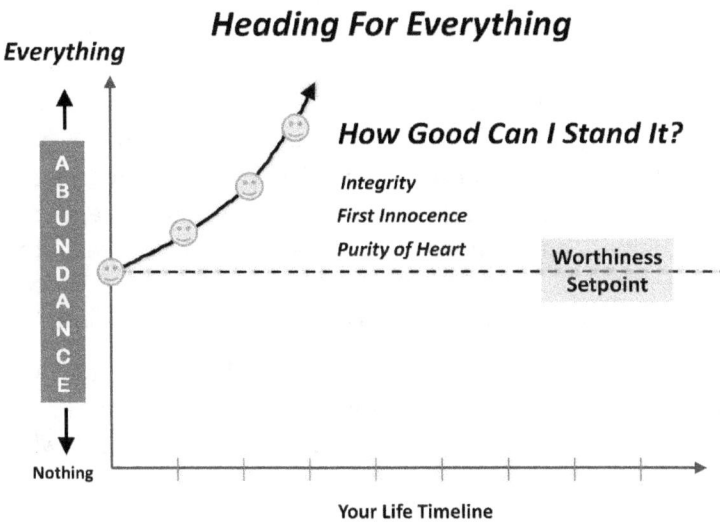

Our Innocence and Value has not had anything piled on top of it yet so we believe that it is a short trip and that we have a direct path to *Everything*. Our innocence on the outside matches our Innocence on the inside. We are happy, and joyous that we are on this adventure and are experiencing more our Innocence and Value as we rise.

The Fear / Attractiveness Dynamic

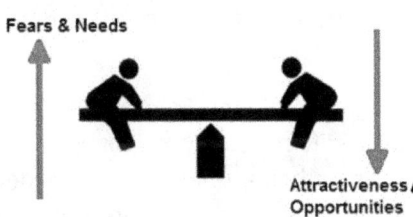

There are two principles that cause us to rise and fall and explain why we gain and lose momentum.

Fear gives off negative energy. We find it heavy and more dense. It is sluggish and feels like a drag on us. We lose **Momentum (MO)** in the presence of Fear. Losing momentum kicks in our survival instinct because if we lose all momentum we are completely vulnerable and will die if momentum cannot be regained.

We move away from Fear both physically and psychologically as quickly as we can. The more Fear we sense the faster we move.

Therefore, the more fear we are in, the less attractive we are to others and to opportunities. This Fear we are in can be overt or covert, meaning that some Fear we know we are in is on the surface, in our outer world. Others can see it. Fear is like an iceberg in that the amount that is overt is only a very small portion of what amount of fear we are actually in.

Covert fear is beneath the surface of our awareness. We can be in a great amount of fear and not really be aware of it. If we have been in intense fear for a long time the body normalized to it and we think 'that's just the way things are. Maybe we aren't sensing our covert fear but others around us do. We can feel it in others. Dogs know it without being told. Covert fear causes us to repel people, opportunities and solutions without knowing why. We seem to have 'bad luck' but it is sub-conscious and unconscious fear that we've never processed and released. Covert Fear causes us to 'lose.'

Winning, in life, with integrity, is positive. The energy it gives off is light, fluid. It feels too good to us and others. We find its energy attractive and invigorating. We move towards people who are Winning and gain momentum as we do.

This creates a self-esteem/self worth feedback loop. The more successes we have in a row, (Wins), the more of our fear melts away. This causes our self-esteem to expand, which dissipates even more fear and makes us even more attractive. Less and less fear means that we become safer to be around. This causes more and better opportunities to be offered to us by people who sense our expanding 'safe to be around' quotient. This facilitates more successes with less and less effort expended, and with it higher self-esteem. We experience this in the world as 'the better things get the better things get.'

Fear shows up as Fight, (attack), Flight, (run), and Freeze, (unable to move or function). We don't necessarily have to be shaking in our boots. Instead fear can show up as us being unable to make decisions, or unable to take risks, or hanging onto a relationship that doesn't serve us. It takes a real sincere effort to find out what fear we are actually broadcasting.

Regardless, if we find people, opportunities and luck moving away from us, it is fear. Fear and Attractiveness, are direct opposites. When fear goes up, attractiveness goes down. When fear goes down your attractiveness goes up, resulting in more Abundance.

It is that simple. If you find yourself unable to attract good things in your life you need to look deeply within for the fear that is hidden inside. If you can't find it go find someone, (counselor, coach, guru, shaman), to help you find it. It is there no matter what your mind is saying to convince you not to look any further.

Then Something Happens!

We continue on this upward trajectory towards *Everything*, experiencing more and more Abundance as we rise.

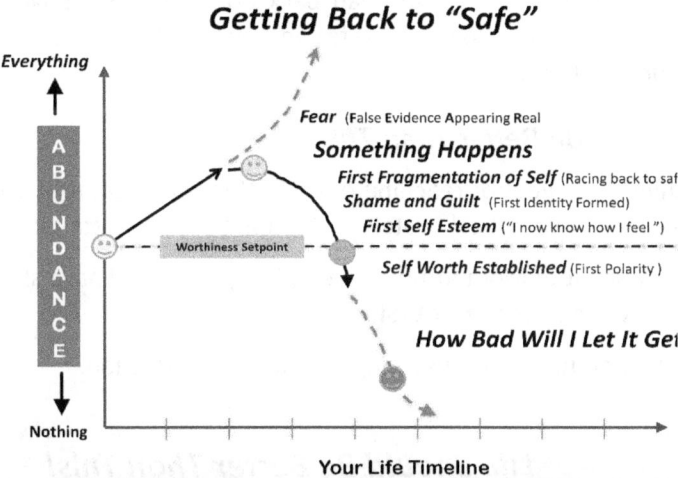

Then **something happens**! We hit an invisible ceiling. Because of our uncontaminated innocence. we didn't even imagine there was such a thing as an upper limit. This *'something'* was an event that blew a hole in us and for some of us blew us into a thousand pieces. Immediately two things happened simultaneously:

- The hole creating by 'something' allows shame, guilt and fear to establish itself within us for the first time.
- Having a hole in our psyche is like a hot air balloon. Because heat, (energy), is escaping through the hole in the balloon it needs more fuel, (efforting), than it did before to rise, (working harder at going out and getting).

This hole remains open until our higher self is brought back to wholeness through healing and forgiveness. Until it is we experience a feeling of Separateness, (no longer connected to our internal world, (Source, The Universe)). Externally this shows up as the belief that the world is now an unsafe place, which results in Fear.

We decide that we are alone in the world and we start protecting and defending ourselves. We feel we are alone and will have to do life on our own (inauthentic independence). With these new assumptions we, quite innocently start erecting the first Walls around our heart making it harder and harder for the Love of others to reach our inner world and the our love, which is stored safely behind the walls.

So with no awareness and experience of such things and with the mind of a child, we decide to abandon our Life Purpose, which would have had us arrive at Everything with ease. *We stop rising towards Everything, turn* and head back down, as fast as we can, towards where we first felt safe and connected... *'our initial Worthiness Setpoint.'*

Life Should Be Better Than This!

We achieve our goal of reaching our Worthiness Setpoint at which time we make two critical mistakes. We don't yet understand:

1. the concept of Momentum. If we did we, we would have slowed as we were nearing our WSP.
2. that a pendulum always swings too far each direction.

Life Should Be Better Than This!

"Life Should be Better Than This!"

Your Life Timeline

We also reason that if 'down' was where we were safe before, then farther down will be *'even more safe.'* This can be compared to us 'eating from the tree of knowledge.'

Before we can put on the breaks we fall past our WSP into a territory we have never experienced before, namely less awareness of Worthiness than we were born with.

This territory is known as "*How Bad Will I let It Get*" which, now with our new-found shame, guilt and fear, will become a familiar place unless we act deliberately. We will need to act in similar circumstances for the rest of our life, sometimes only with our sheer will as our friend.

In the territory "*How Bad Will I let It Get*", as we drop farther away from our Worthiness Setpoint, we begin to lose the influence of our innate innocence. We begin to accept the idea that we are somehow guilty and a 'sinner'. The pull of our Worthiness Setpoint becomes less and less. We discover ourselves attracted to *Nothing*.

"*How Bad Will I Let It Get*" is a territory where we are so far from *Everything* (Love and Connection) that we are now expending greater and greater energy units just to stay alive.

Our Second Greatest Fear

As we head lower and gain a greater distance from our Worthiness Set Point we move from Getting and Giving and into 'Taking and Grabbing.' We are now taking more energy out of the world than we are putting in and heading hell bent towards our own personal Ground Zero. Momentum at this point is no longer our friend

Our Second Greatest Fear (2GF)

As we get closer and closer to Nothing we begin to experience for the first time the second greatest fear in the human mind, (2GF), one that is deeply engrained in our emotional DNA.

This is the fear of merging completely with 'Nothing.' which translates into our fear of the total absence of feeling and therefore being totally 'Numb', Nothing also represents to us the thoughts and feelings of being completely off Purpose.

Oliver Wendell Holmes said **"Many people die with their music still in them"** and the thought of that degree of numbness is so out of integrity and most of the time causes us to expend huge amounts of energy to pull out of the bottom of the loop before we crash into Nothing. We all know of people who didn't have the energy or means to counter their fears, regrets, self loathing, revenge and judgments and leave this world too early.

'Everything' is Greater Than 'Nothing'

If we do manage to break our fall and round through the bottom of the loop we begin to feel the intense attraction of Everything. At this low point in our worthiness cycle the upward pull of Everything has never been as intense. We begin to pick up momentum from our desire to join with *Everything*.

Too much momentum will always turn out to be a bad thing no matter whether you are heading towards what you don't want or attracted to what you do want.

So the same thing happens again. We attempt to grab on and stay at our safest point, our worthiness Setpoint, and again, we can't hold back. We don't even really try because we know that Everything is where the purest love and connection is.

But as almost all really successful people who have 'fallen from grace' with tell you, it is dangerous to rise too fast without taking the time to establish a new worthiness Setpoint, getting on firm footing and experiencing Safety at that new location higher up the mountain. This explains completely why so many who win the Lotto have very little of it left after a few years.

As we rise, picking up speed like a home sick angel, we reach a point along the journey of more abundance than we have experienced before. We rise higher than we've ever been before. We have now entered completely new territory on the upside of our worthiness Setpoint, known as the "How Good Can I Stand It?" Zone.

The Different Feelings Above and Below Our WSP

When we were down in 'How Bad Will I let it Get', we learned what confusion, frustration, disappointment and despair feels like. You would think that rising into How Good Can You Stand It would be free of negative feelings but not so fast truth seeker. In this place you feel more 'enlightened' than you have ever felt before, but you also feel intense amounts of anxiety, doubt, sadness, valuelessness, and what I call *'Emotional Heat.'*

Emotional Heat

Emotional Heat is the result of rising too quickly, skipping over a full understanding of the lessons we need to learn in this part of our journey. We must learn a new and deeper understanding of attributes required to rise into the How Good zone AND stay there. 'Patience' is one example of a personal attribute required. Unless we have a higher understanding of Patience we are likely to be seen praying this prayer: "Dear God, please give me Patience and, respectively give it to me RIGHT NOW!" and perplexed because we are experiencing a lot of emotional heat, 'learning', patience.

As we put greater distance between us and our fear of Numbness we start to make more and more progress faster and faster, we do find that, 'perfect', life partner. We do get that really good paying job and we pay off the mortgage. We finally have the time and money to go on real holidays to exciting places. We garner more and more respect from family, friends, our peers and the community in which we are contributing very fulfilling service work. All is wonderful, great, fantastic, couldn't be better, (except for this feeling that keeps gnawing at me).

Don't Get Too Abundant and Make God Mad

However, all is not well in the realm of Abundance. As <u>Miceal Ledwith</u> of the movie "What The Bleep Do We Know" says: "a worry starts to fester within us." We worry that if we get too happy, contented and abundant we are going to attract the attention of the angry narcissistic cruel and punishing god we have all been indoctrinated to believe in. This version god has been shoved down our throats for centuries by everyone pretending to be holy. Ledwith speaks of this being so engrained in our psyche that we all pause at this part in our evolution.

While this worry that the other shoe will drop soon gains momentum we level out and temper our climb a bit, but the gravitational pull of Everything is so great that we really can't resist the attraction of that Abundance.

"Oh My God!"

As we get closer to Everything we suddenly gain awareness of something that just completely terrifies us.

It is something we will always run away from, usually by some act we know will save us like having an affair, losing all our retirement money to someone we knew all along was a sham artist, getting deathly ill and a million other things when we've reached the place this time around the cycle where we 'can't stand it any better.' The thing we get a glimpse of that terrifies us is actually the greatest fear in our human mind.

As we do our healing work and peel away all the layers of protection and personalities we accumulated since our first experience of *'forget everything and run'*, We begin to have the awareness of 'our true self' where we are increasingly capable of allowing Abundance both internally and externally. We know we have never been this joyous, fulfilled and connected. We have a 'knowingness' that are closer to our center than every before and it is so filled with happiness and fulfillment that we commit to never returning to lower realms of our initial WSP. It is at this point that we come face to face with something we couldn't even imagine was there. Suddenly we gain our first realization of the one and only thing that will cause us to run away from this high place. One that we will always run away from until we don't.

> *"We are all capable of becoming fundamentalists because we get addicted to other people's wrongness."*
>
> ~ Pema Chödrön

Our Single Greatest Fear (1GF)

The greatest fear in the human mind is ***The Fear Of Having It All.***

Marianne Williamson, said it best (often attributed to Nelson Mandela) when she wrote in 'A Return To Love':

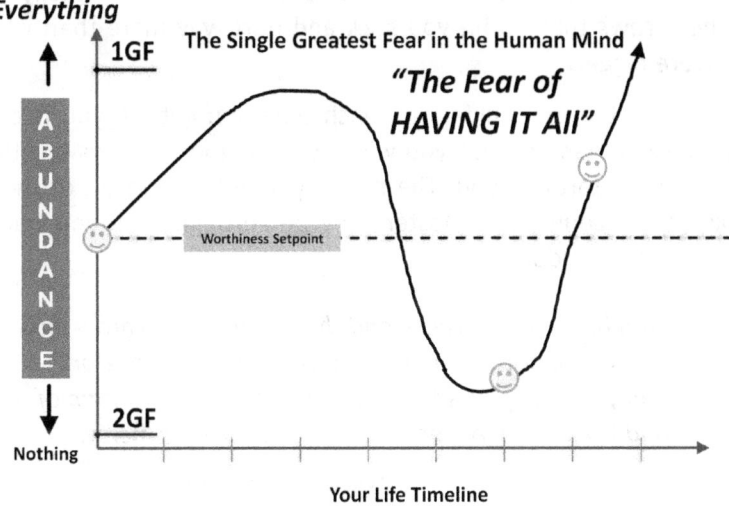

"Our deepest fear is not that we are inadequate. Our deepest fear is that we are powerful beyond measure. It is our light, not our darkness that most frightens us.

~ Marianne Williamson

Our Greatest Fear can be expressed this way: It is our fear that we are made "of God, not by God", (Now don't let your mind make a big deal of the word God... you can call it the Higher Mind...The Universe... Great Spirit, or Frank. it's not important what you call it. Here I call it **Everything)**.

So the Worthiness Cycle is the primal of all of life's ups and downs. We rise and fall reacting to our two greatest fears. Rising makes us lighter where our atoms of energy and information, as Deepak would say, move farther apart from each other. Travelling down makes us heavier and heavier. Hanging around Nothing makes one dense and all our atoms move closer together for protection.

This understanding provides us with a new way to view how we show up in the world. At first we are wide open to everything that comes at us. Then we take a few hits from arrows that hurt as they go through. Our humanness tells us to crouch down, make ourselves small and less of a target.

While it is true that you do get hit by fewer arrows you are much denser when you have made yourself smaller than you actually are, so the arrows that do hit you stick and hurt way more than when you were bigger.

If you have the mindfulness to, each time you get hit, you rise up and make yourself bigger, you will get hit by more arrows but they will sail right through you. The bigger you get as a result of the attacks you encounter the faster they go through until you hardly notice when one does.

> *I am here for a purpose and that purpose is to grow into a mountain, not to shrink to a grain of sand. Henceforth will I apply all my efforts to become the highest mountain of all and I will strain my potential until it cries for mercy.*
>
> *~ Og Mandino*

Below the Survival Line we are in **"How Bad Will I Let it Get?"**

"How much will I allow my personality, judgments and beliefs take me before I realize I'm trying to be killed off by my own run away eMaEo?"(eMaEo (pronounced 'me') - eMaEo stands for 'Easing More and Everything out.'

On the higher side of your perceived level of Thriving in "How Good Can I Stand it?" we are asking ourselves how much abundance can I let in before I allow anxiety to have me stop and head for 'the valley of the shadow of death?'

Our Worthiness Cycle is Life Long

Until we understand and integrate the Worthiness Cycle into our personality we return again and again to the most counterproductive characteristic of human beings: *"Doing more of the same expecting different results."*

> *"If you do what you've always done, you'll get what you've always gotten"*
>
> *~ **Anthony Robbins***

Addiction – The Opposite of Abundance

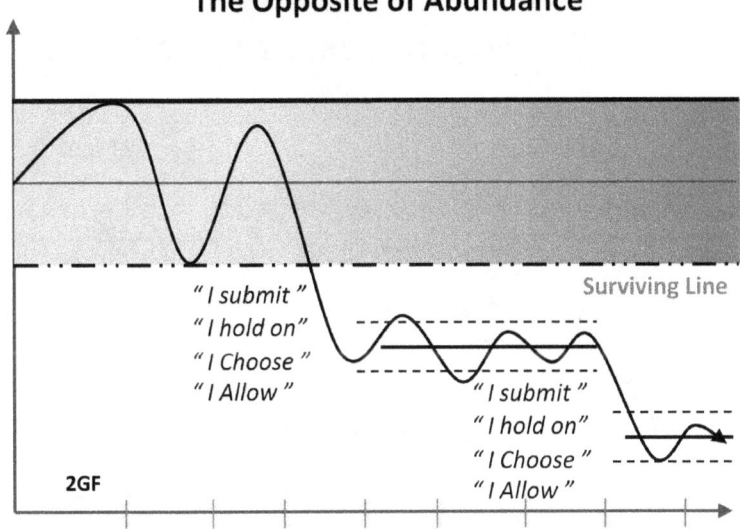

The Addiction Cycle
The Opposite of Abundance

As we accumulate more and more Shame, Guilt, Fear, Loss and Hurt, we have to do something to handle all the negative energy they generate, so we reach for relief and comfort. It could be Booze, Drugs, Sex, Snowboarding, Food, TV, Travel, Worry, Poor Health or all of them at the same time. It doesn't matter which, they are all addictions when we reach for them to give us relief from our pain.

Once we receive relief from something often enough it becomes a habit, then a trend, then a pattern, then an addiction, then a cause of death. First the Rolex goes, then the car, then the job, then the wife and kids, then the furniture, the house, the clothing and then

It looks like this: We come over the top, getting away from our greatest fear, head down into "How Bad Will I Let It Get", establish a new Worthiness Setpoint, get comfortable with this much Abundance, then head down further and repeat that pattern until we are standing in front of Nothing. At this point we must choose.

Choice points

Choose to get beyond our fear of Nothing, round the corner, and head back up towards Abundance or choose to succumb to Nothing and DIE. You might have come to this point already, but if you haven't, you will. When you have succumbed to whatever it is that gives you comfort from your pain you will. We all do.

Allowing Ever Increasing Abundance

The Empowerment Cycle

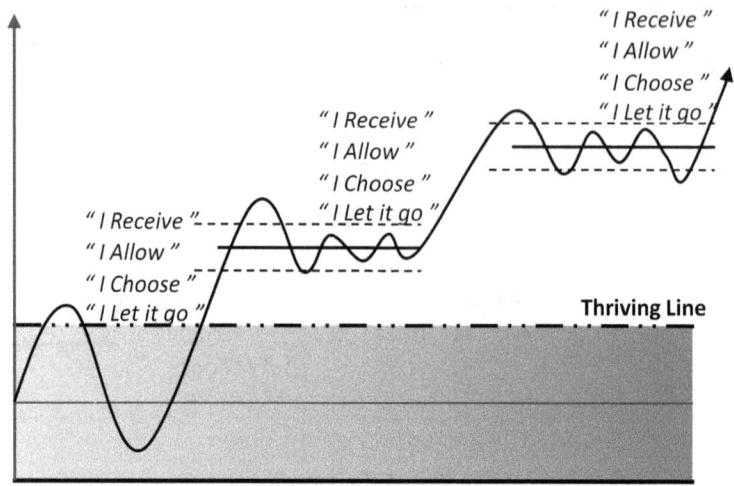

The good news is that being Abundant is Addiction in Reverse. Rising up, receiving more Abundance, overcoming the anxiety of Receive, getting comfortable then allowing yourself to do it again and again.

If you can be addicted, and we all are, you have the software in place to create Abundance.

The only difference is that on the down side you 'grab' less and less of life (grasping at straws) and on the up side you allow yourself to overcome anxiety and the emotional heat of Receive, and allow more and more Abundance. It's simply a change in perception.

At first some nice things start to happen to you. You get a good job, meet someone interesting, get married, get promoted, have a beautiful baby, gain acceptance and respect of your parents, family and community. Any one of these things happening will reduce your 'needs' and therefore your fears and you will naturally start to rise. The fewer your needs the more attractive you are, the more you attract into your life, the more Abundance you receive with ease.

"Fear is a natural reaction to moving closer to the truth"

~ Pema Chödrön

***Abundance Anxiety* (AA)** is something we experience when we are receiving more attention, riches, love than we are able to take in without losing control of the situation and being completely overwhelmed. It is our attempt to control a situation that would make us totally vulnerable. Abundance Anxiety is at the root of all addictions.

The faster you overcome your Abundance Anxiety the sooner you rise to the next level of Worthiness. The more levels you allow yourself to rise through the more you receive and the closer you get to 1GF - the greatest fear you have closest to your core. But every level of Worthiness comes with either the capacity to tolerate less and less or the capability of dealing with The Greatest Fear.

This is the same for salesmen, teams, companies and organizations. The Worthiness Cycle shows us a Universal truth.

And now for one of the most ironic things in the Universe:

Where we lost sight of our innate innocence and value, and accumulated all these limiting beliefs, thoughts, judgments and fears is the same place where we can rise through them the fastest.

> *We mere mortals call this. 'Relationships.'*

Worthiness And Relationships

All Hurts, Wounds, Abandonment, Abuse and Betrayals happen within the realm of Relationship.

All arguments, grievances and wars happen in Relationships so I suppose it's not all that ironic that Relationship is where we will find our salvation.

In every relationship we have ever had, or will have, we are in effect overlaying our Worthiness cycle over someone else's. Both parties don't merge into one Cycle but remain two and the interaction of the two cycles determines how the relationship functions.

> *"Find someone who is heading in the right direction, someone who scares the hell out of you, and marry them!"*

Mistakes That Cost Us Our Life

Every hurt, disappointment and argument that you have ever had and the resulting grievance that you now carry locked within you is the result of only a few things that are simply mistakes.

- Not recognizing where you are on the Worthiness Cycle, and how you got there.
- Not rising and falling at the same rate as someone else.
- Not recognizing where the other person is on the Cycle.
- Not responding from a place of Mindfulness to the pressures of being in different places with different ideas of success and happiness.
- Knowing the direction to head and not following or being held back
- Insisting on what direction someone should be heading.
- Not recognizing when you or the other person have hit Fear and have changed direction.
- Not being able to pull someone or yourself out of a dive.
- Watching them crash through their life timeline and die.
- Needing to travel your road less traveled "all by yourself" because it's just easier that way.
- Being unwilling to leave the comfort zone.
- Dragging someone into the Dead Zone because of your fears.
- Watching someone head for How Bad Will I let It Get?
- Feeling left behind as someone rises in new levels of Abundance.
- Being ashamed because you got scared and turned away from people, career and investments that you knew was leading you to Abundance.

And perhaps the most clever of them all...

Knowing enough about all this to set it up so that you use someone else to hold you back from Abundance and then make them guilty for it.

The NOT So Comfortable Zone

The Three Zones of Discomfort

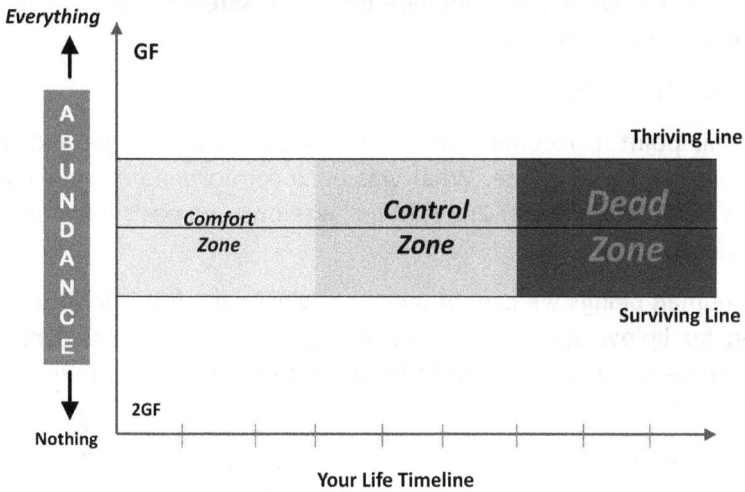

As we go up and down a few times, through our Worthiness Cycle, we establish a pattern within a certain range above and below our initial Worthiness Setpoint.

You establish two other Setpoints, a line at the top of your highest peaks, called the *"Thriving Line"* and at the bottom of your lowest regular turn around points called the *"Survival Line."* This newly formed area represents the average amount of Abundance we can tolerate and the average amount of Lack that we can tolerate beneath our original WSP. We all know this as our *'Comfort Zone'*.

The Comfort Zone

The Comfort Zone establishes itself once we have traveled through the Cycle a few times. As we all know, the more we stay in it the more we use it to keep our life under control. Our comfort zone is the way we protect ourselves from Fear and Pain. The problem is that is also protects us from Abundance as well.

"I've got to get in control of my life" is a common saying. The problem with it is that the more we stay in the Comfort Zone the less we are able to feel and experience in life.

We use the same strategies for our safety and abundance that we have learned work for us most of the time. Naturally these strategies for living become habits and eventually, because we are now a different person in a different stage, with different circumstances, begin to lose their effectiveness.

What once made things in our life better, now either has little or no effect and often makes things worse. What was initially the Comfort Zone where we felt an adequate degree of safety starts to have its own influence, taking on a life of its own.

The Control Zone

At this point it becomes harder and harder to break free and rise above our Thriving Line. What was once comfortable morphs itself into being *'the Control Zone'*. What was once an oasis has now become a prison.

As human beings we cannot avoid growing, even if it is in little bits and far below our potential. Watching TV for four hours a night, seven days a week is going to teach us something even if we don't want it to.

Over time we become more expansive but our Control Zone isn't getting any bigger unless we force it to, which we do not have the awareness to do or we wouldn't be hanging around in the Control Zone in the first place.

Like our bodies, even though we are replacing some cells, if we are not replacing old cells with new cells fast enough, we are actually dying. As we are growing and our Control Zone is not getting any larger it has the effect of reducing the energy we have for living.

The Dead Zone

'What the hell is the use?' becomes our theme and dis-ease sets in, the most common being Depression.

We are now in the final and most restrictive zone of our life, *'the Dead Zone.'* There is not much going on, everything feels heavy and uninspiring. Many people never make it out of the Dead Zone. They die, not for any known scientific reason, but as a strategy to get out of the Dead Zone. Suicide does not occur to us as a strategy until we are in the Dead Zone.

High Effort and Energy Demand

It takes effort and energy to stay in the Comfort Zone because something is always calling to us to rise up and come to Everything. It takes even more energy, robbing us of the excitement and pleasure that would invigorate us, to stay in the Control Zone.

Once we move into the Dead Zone it is going to take a significant event that is full of energy to be able to break out of the Dead Zone. Somebody like a therapist, life coach or soul mate has to come in and get us, but because we're so deadish and uninspired we are not attractive. We don't find too many soul mates willing to sign up for the job.

On the Menu Tonight 'Deep Fried Human'

It is as if we have made our way into a hot tub. It is warm, comforting and refreshing for a few minutes. Unbeknown to us, behind a tree are a tribe of cannibals turning up the heat a little bit at a time. As they turn up the heat gradually we begin to lose our desire and will to get out of the hot tub, especially because our 'server' is bringing us ice cold water to quench our thirst. In the Control Zone, we get just enough refreshment, variety and excitement to not notice what is happening.

As the heat is turned up ever so slowly, we don't notice our overall capacity to lift ourselves out of the hot tub is diminished and dropping. By this time our server has begun to bring us trays full of Margaritas with cute little umbrellas poking out the top. We think we're having a party.

In the Control Zone we find artificial boosters like booze, drugs or food to relieve the discomfort and boredom and make life tolerable. Our intuition tries to tell us that we are selling ourselves short and are going to die if we don't change course and fast. But we override it and pay little attention because Death has now signed the lease and moved in so we can become familiar with it.

At this point the cannibals know that they need do nothing but wait because our strength and desire to get out of the tub is all but gone and the margaritas have put us to sleep. We are soon somebody's feast, listed on the menu as 'Dumb Asleep Human, Roasted In A Nice Light Wine Sauce.'

Never Take Your Eyes Off The Prize

We all need to stop and take a break. Hanging out in our Comfort Zone for awhile is necessary. Some of us mistake the Comfort Zone as our enemy and never take a break. We call them *'workaholics'* and society rewards them with a lot of 'atta boy's' but what is really going on is that they are compensating for shame and guilt. Work is one of the best ways we've found for avoiding Success.

The Circle Song by Joni Mitchell talks about the dead zone as the ups and downs of life where we get trapped on a carousel going round and round, never going anywhere and never getting off.

> Sixteen springs and sixteen summers gone now
> Cartwheels turn to car wheels thru the town
> And they tell him take your time it won't be
> long now Till you drag your feet to slow the
> circles down
>
> And the seasons they go round and round
> And the painted ponies go up and down
> We're captive on the carousel of time
> We can't return we can only look
> Behind from where we came
> And go round and round and round
> In the circle game

But very quickly after we have caught our breath and had a good massage (both mind and body) in our comfort zone we must develop strategies, a non-negotiable timetable and action plan for when we are going to leave before we get a bit 'too comfortable.' Tony Robbins's *Unlimited Power* weekend seminar is one of the best ways to break free from comfort, control and dead zones.

Insisting on Being Right

The Rightitudes

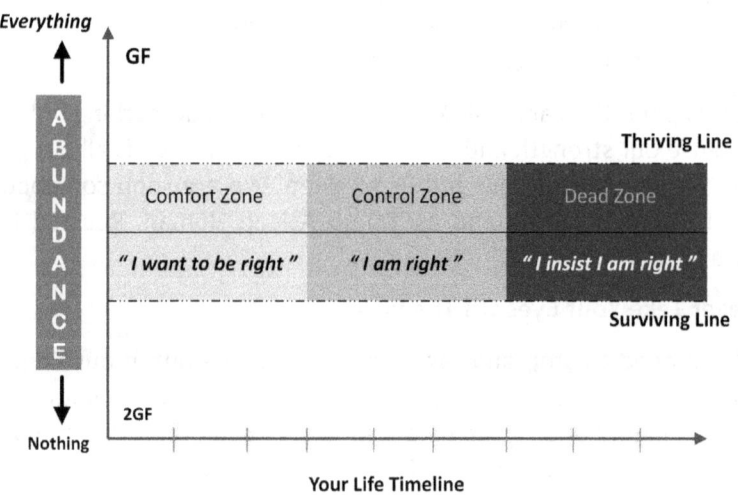

One of the things that facilitates us leaving our Comfort Zone and sliding into the Control Zone is that we have made something more important than our purposeful fulfillment.

The theme of our lives has become *"I wanta be right:"*

> "I wanta be right that "he/she" is not the one for me."
>
> "I wanta be right that my company is not the one in which to make my stand."
>
> "I wanta be right that the government is doing it to me."
>
> "I wanta be right that "my mother" is beyond hope."
>
> "I wanta be right that I'm not smart enough."
>
> "I wanta be right that my obesity is genetic."

And the best avoider of success, happiness and fulfillment is...

> ***"I want to be right that he/she/they have done me wrong and owe me an apology and I'm not going to move one more step forward in my life until I get it."***

(I know you yourself have never got caught in that one but you've seen people in your family that have one as their problem.)

In counseling we say: **"you can be right or you can be happy, but you can't be both."** Some of us want to be right so much that we don't care if we are happy, just as long as the other person is less happy than we are.

Keeping Ourselves Safe and Small

> *"Our ability to allow and receive, in every area of our life, is directly related to our ability to forgive"*

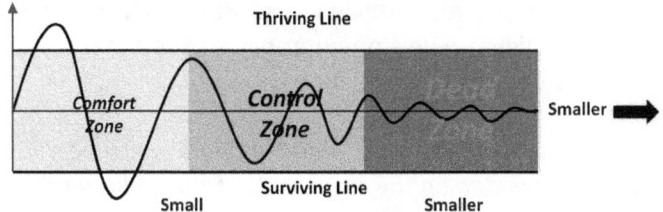

Gathered Evidence to Support Discomfort

One of the reasons that we end up in the Comfort Zone in the first place is that we begin to 'hide out' from life. Over time, as we go up and down through the Cycle enough times, we begin to gather evidence that our life is "just the way it is" and we begin to settle for less than it can be.

While that could be true because it's been our life experience, it is not the end of the story.

In life, we only have to pick ourselves up more times than we stay down to be successful. If you're still walking around on the planet you are more successful than those you knew in high school.

Just because you've never seen or experienced something doesn't mean it isn't true.

> *The Way' it is, is only the way it is... for now!"*

(Add **'for now'** to any statement you make about yourself that holds you hostage. It is a great 'pattern interrupter'.)

The actual truth is that if you rise and stay above the thriving line long enough, you'll gather enough evidence and get comfortable there, and capture a new level of Worthiness and Abundance. If you remain down in the muck of 'life should be better than this,' you gather similar evidence and learn how to be comfortable at that level. The choice is, of course, always yours. Some of us get addicted to being outside of our Comfort Zone and below the Survival line. Physiologists say these people are "addicted to their own pain."

Get Familiar, Comfortable And Confident

> *"If you are not willing to risk the unusual, you will have to settle for the ordinary."*
>
> ~ Jim Rohn

A word of caution. You can and should rise above your Thriving line and remain there until you feel safe and comfortable. New Comfort Zones at higher and higher levels on your way to Everything is the only way to create sustainable Abundance.

> *"And on the seventh day God ended his work which he had made; and he rested on the seventh day from all his work which he had made."*

Even God took a break once he/she had established a new level of Worthiness.

Of course it's just as easy to establish a new Comfort Zone below your Surviving line, establishing new levels of 'Less and Lack', which is not your birthright or your purpose, but you have enough willpower to make that happen if you insist.

Worthiness Filters and Blind Spots

Your Worthiness Filters

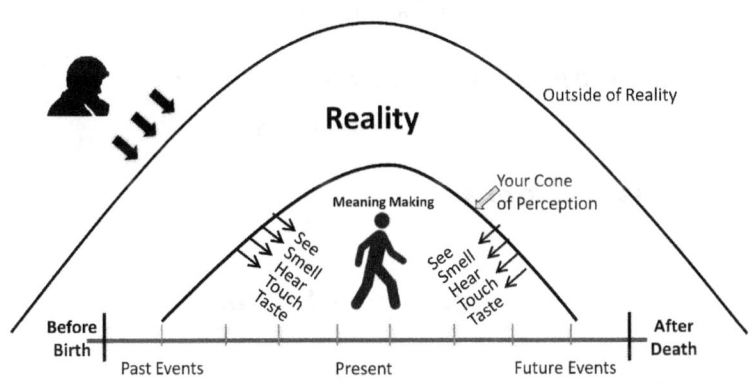

Your Life Events Timeline

After we have firmly imprinted this Cycle into our subconscious mind we develop what I call *"worthiness filters."* Our Worthiness Filter is located just below our conscious awareness. It is like a lens through which we view our entire construct of reality.

Everything we believe, everything passes through our Worthiness Filter. It's objective is make judgments to keep us safe. While this was helpful initially it doesn't serve us now in rising into Abundance.

Unfortunately it *'always'* us gives false readings because it filters everything through every assumption, judgment and decision we made in the past whether accurate, or not. It continually provides us evidence that the safest place for us to be is in our Comfort Zone.

Survival, Safety and Conquest

The Worthiness Filter is our attempt to see bad things coming at us before they actually arrive and then cause changes in our beliefs and actions that will return us to safety.

As a result, we often miss making a good choice consciously or unconsciously. We will walk by someone instead of striking up a conversation, not because they weren't our soul mate but because they WERE! but didn't look like it because of the Filter .We 'forget' about that job we saw in the paper that was 'meant for me' or we don't mail our resume on time or it's 'not organized' when we do send it, so as to make sure that they won't hire us.

This is how we create our lives. Often we think that we are just living in a bunch of circumstances but as you can see, you are far more in control of your life than you thought and that's GOOD NEWS, because if you are in control of it by your thoughts and actions, you can actually catch yourself through awareness and change it. You are only a victim when you remain asleep.

> *"Nothing in its essence is one way or the other."*
>
> ~ Pema Chödrön

Worthiness Meltdowns

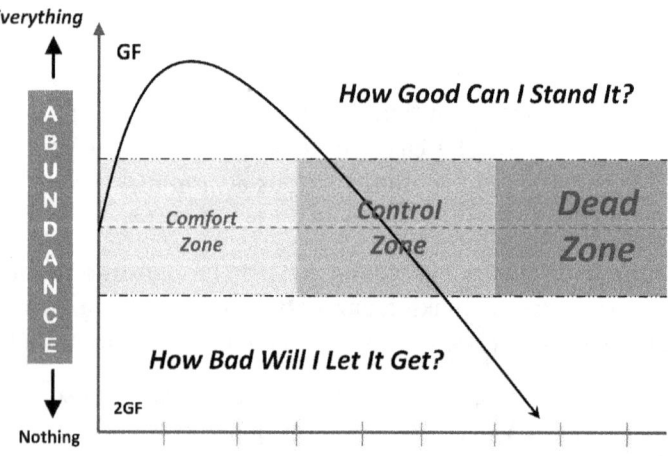

> *"Most of man's difficulties comes from his inability, to sit quietly... in a room... alone"*
>
> ~ Pascal

An interesting thing happens once you become aware of worthiness. Life starts becoming abundant and you start getting lighter and lighter. You say things like "*I feel like a load has just been lifted off my shoulders.*" Abundance does that to a person.

All of a sudden, you'll find yourself heading for Nothing faster than you ever have before and you can't find the reason. **"Damn, just** *when I was feeling so light too; I guess all this rising to Everything is just a bunch of bull shit so I'm going to fogetaboutit."*

Meltdown is our fear of losing control and just dissolving into a bundle of happiness right now without warning. Said another way It is our fear of becoming 'a ball of light' and then *'going 'everywhere all at once.'*

To realize that you now have the capacity to see *'beyond the veil'* is to know that you are in a major transformational stage. But you don't want to doff your Armani suit just yet. You are fearful when this transformation is complete you'll be wearing robs without pants, clothes that only hippies and weirdoes wear. EMaEo has without notice frantically taken control. (it does this now because at this level it's power over you is substantially less and it things that 'it' might lose total control and die.)

Indicators A Meltdown Immanent

We never experience Worthiness Meltdown when we are feeling weak, venerable and depressed. A full blown Meltdown, activated only when we are getting much closer to *'Everything.'* Worthiness Meltdowns are so insidious because it only activates when you're feeling GREAT, more fantastic than we've ever felt before.

A Worthiness Meltdown Step By Step

We find ourselves making many breakthroughs, rising quickly to new heights of Abundance. Our Worthiness quotient and have been rising into more Abundance for quite a long time. Without any notice we suddenly become more anxious than we ever have before. A well camouflaged layer has suddenly reveals itself that has us believing that we got this high by mistake. We strongly suspect we rose to this height because all the way along we have been fooling everyone including ourselves. Secretly we suspect that we even did a con job on God and there will be 'hell to pay' when he finds out.

We become convinced that the incredible amounts of joy, freedom and connection we have just begun to experience is beyond what is fair, right and sustainable. Our good friend eMaEo has been whispering to us, saying that it won't last and that very soon we will be terribly alone again.

Fear and doubt rises very quickly to a level higher and more intense that ever been before. With all we've learned, processed, healed, integrated and let go of, we can't stop it from increasing in intensity and that makes us feel deeply ashamed. We reason "this must be the place where God has become very mad at me for thinking I deserved such Abundance. Terrible , un-survivable punishment is emanate any moment now." The combination of intense fear, shame, guilt and mistrust convinces us to turn and run for safety faster than we have ever done before.

Meltdown Stems From Our 'Fear of Greatness

We sometimes see this as someone who was an executive on a fast track to the top of the company and then next time you see him, he's sleeping on a park bench and drinking wine out of a bottle in a paper bag.

Most of us see homeless people and say *"what a shame, if they only knew how valuable they actually are."* What if they had actually seen their true value once and didn't have the awareness and skills to stay up where they belong and so the ran at lightening speed for safer realms.

'There but for the grace of God go I'

At some level higher than where you are today you don't have those skills either. Understanding the Worthiness Cycle and what impact it has on your life is the first step in being able to soak up Abundance when it's coming at you faster than you can control.

Counter Balancers to Worthiness

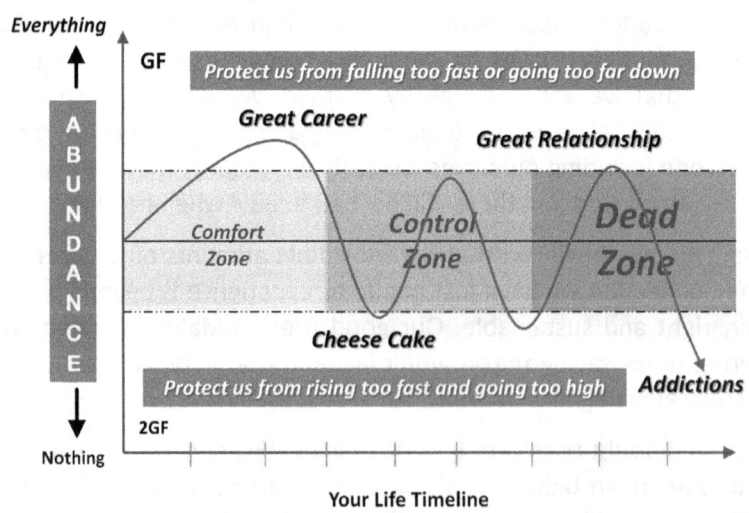

For all of the reasons stated above we are afraid or being 'too' great and we are afraid of being 'too' nothing. Being as clever as we are we put people and situations in place to make sure that we will never have to deal with too much Fear or Anxiety.

Counter Balancers are the things we use on one side of our Worthiness Setpoint to hold back something on the other side. It's the way we keep from being too abundant in several areas at the same time.

My favorite one is food. I can have a great relationship going on and my career is really getting abundant but I can't seem to stop eating hamburgers and French fries with gravy at least once a day.

Every morning I stand in front of the mirror and remind myself of the promise I made myself I wouldn't have another fast food meal.

Every night I let in the thought that I am a weakling and how I don't deserve to have everything that life has to offer because I went back on my word. Shame, guilt, negative self talk are my eMaEo's way of keeping everything nice and comfortable!

In this way we are responsible for a lot of the negative situations and 'catch 22's' we find ourselves in.

After many years of feeling like a victim I have begun to entertain the idea that we create 'every' situation, problem, challenge that we ever have. This doesn't necessarily mean that you created 'the exact' situation but were operating in such a way that 'something of that type and intensity of a problem' was in the neighborhood and willing to step up the minute we presented an opportunity.

1. What people, situations and events have you put in place to protect you from feeling Anxious or Afraid?
2. What people, situations and events have you put in place to protect you from Abundance?

Core Principles of Worthiness

Everything Wants To Live For Ever

In the race between the lion and the zebra one is going to survive and one is going to die. That is the way of things and it's always been that way.

When you watch this play out on the National Geographic Channel on TV it's hard to know how to feel. We celebrate the one who has gathered the sustenance they must have for their basic survival. We mourn the one that has had the life drained out of them until they are no longer here.

Who you cheer for gives you a clue to the strategies that you employ to survive and from which your worthiness quotient rises and falls. The intensity of the survival instinct is easily understood in the animal kingdom. Somehow deep inside us we know how both the winner and the loser feels.

Everything in the Universe that has energy wants to stay alive and thrive. That includes us, the **animals** of course and even **plants** which we watch grow through the thinnest crack in the sidewalk.

Bugs want to stay alive. Microbes we can only see in our world with a microscope want to stay alive just as much.

Viruses in our blood stream insist on staying alive. Look how hard it has been to find a cure for the common cold.

Habits insist on staying alive. Ideas of ours and everyone else's have energy so they want to live forever. Energy is not discerning. They all want to live no matter whether 10,000 years old or something that popped into our head an hour ago.

Both the most horrid of **ideas** about how to torture and the ideas that flow past our mind as we read a poem, are equal in that neither has any shame or reasons of their own for their own expiration. An Ideas don't care if it is good or a bad. Only humans decide that and we change our minds without reason or regard to logic or value.

Memories want to stay alive. Memories literally glue themselves onto synapses inside the neural networks in our brain to such extent that it can take a lifetime to unhook them from our being.

Thoughts want to stay alive. Good thoughts, bad thoughts, even the ones that want to kill us. Those thoughts gather and communicate evidence that they deserve to survive just as much as the lion does.

> **Worthiness Principle - Give your thoughts the same respect that you give the lion. Both will try and eat us if they have to in order to survive.**

Life is a Cycle Not A Struggle

Native Americans have long held the tradition that we should view our life in terms of a thousand years. In that perspective some centuries you're winning and some decades you're losing. Within those thousand years you have been the good, the bad, the ugly and the beautiful many times over.

A business writer was interviewing the founder of Sony for an article on Planning.

"Does Sony have a plan for its business?" he asked.

"Of course" the founder said.

"How long does it look ahead?" the writer asked to get the conversation started.

"500 years" was the reply.

"FIVE HUNDRED YEARS? My god what do you need to follow a 500 year business plan?" the startled reporter asked?

"Patience" Mr. Sony replied softly with confidence…. *"Patience."*

In our world stocks of public traded companies can swing widely up and down just from a bad quarterly earnings report. Who is going to win the competition for customers in the end? Mr. Sony? I'm pretty sure yes.

We operate within dozens of cycles at all times - astrological, biological and psychological. And they are never in harmony with each other, when one is up another is down.

When a cycle needs another cycle to be up, but it is down, all kinds of bells start ringing. Change must happen immediately. At any given point in the cycle you can stop and make a decision and declare what's going on is, either good or bad, right or wrong, heaven or hell.

This is what Judgments are, a declaration that something is a certain way and that way is the right way. But a year, a week, a day, an hour, a second ago it could have been exactly the opposite, ecstatic one minute and in the depths of despair the next.

> ***Judgment is so damaging and completely opposite from where you will find Worthiness.***

In slowing down we get to see more of each thought as it goes by. We can understand more fully and accurately what was really going on and how we should respond to have the best possible outcome. Worthiness is located in the space between our thoughts and feelings.

One line of code in the software of our brains does only one thing and one thing only... every single millisecond of every thought, feeling, action or observation it asks only one question:

Do you want this to continue? Yes or no?

Every second that is between every word in any argument we answer Yes or No. Both have consequences in every areas of our life from now until the day we die. We have interrupted a theme and a pattern and every Cycle has to make adjustments accordingly.

If we say yes, our stomach immediately stars to produce more acid. If we say no we have decreased our chances of dying from a heart attack by a significant percentage. Our answer is going to invoke an answer from the person we are arguing with and therefore we have decreased or increased their chance of having a heart attack as well.

This awareness is where 'taking total responsibility' for our choices is found. There we will find our Worthiness as well.

> **Worthiness Principle - Live each moment in the Cycle not in the Struggle**

We Are Committed To Both Success and Failure

We all experience bursts of fresh energy that come to us when we have a success. We can call this Everything Good, which is a place of abundance that knows it can share its energy with you because it has lots of it and gets more than it needs all the time.

We also know what it feels like to lose energy when we have a failure. We feel like we have stuck our finger in a wall socket and had the failure almost suck the very life right out of us. Something draws that energy because we feel it when it's gone. It has gone somewhere and that 'somewhere' is prepared to take all that we are able and willing to give until we have no more left. It makes sense to call this place 'Nothing Good.'

The more success we have the more energy we get. The more failures we have the more depleted we become. I'm not making this up. These ideas are based upon a book called "Power Versus Force," by David R. Hawkins.

Now here's the insidious part. Failure disguises itself as good ideas that will lead to Success. It paints over the rust and sells us a 'bucket of bolts' car. It tells us smoking is good for us because it feels good. It tells us that whiskey tastes just as good as ice cream. It tells us that drugs are really a spiritual experience we should explore. It tells us that a job that we intuitively know we will hate, is the right job for us and it tells us that every morning for the next 20 years. It camouflages mean-spirited people as potential life partners and vicious arguments as a 'good way to blow off some steam.'

Failure builds us up with small successes so that we have lots of energy and then tricks us into disappointment after disappointment so it can feed. But it doesn't want to have us fail all the way because if we die it dies. Eckhart Tolle calls it The Pain Body. A Course in Miracles calls it The Ego. Many religions call it The Devil. Obi-Wan Kenobi called it *"The Dark Side"*

It's known by many other names. I have given it the name 'Nothing' because it takes everything in its path and gives nothing back. Nothing is a place where we feel numb, not worth anything, of no value, totally shattered and exhausted. I tell the truth in my seminar when I say that:

"When I was the closest to Nothing that I've ever been I would have shot myself but I didn't care enough or have enough energy to get up off the couch and go across the room to get the bullet." Nothing is represented as Failure and Everything is represented by Success.

The Games of Failure and Success

Failure and Success are constantly at war and their battleground lie within ourselves. The only prisoners they take are us. They both have about the same power, with Success having the upper hand unless we allow Failure to feed on us too often.

We feel the effects in each of the battles as renewed life force or exhaustion. We have to deal with the results in our outer world, the world of our family, friends, team mates, achievements or lack thereof. All of this remains, for the most part, completely out of our awareness. We finance the war all by ourselves so is it any wonder that we're tired all the time?

We never see it until we decide to take the steps to rise up into a level of consciousness where it gradually becomes clear as day.

Failure has a vested interest in keeping us down because it steals energy whereas Success gives it willingly. Failure has to be smarter and more strategic because it has to keep you hopeful enough so that you get energy from Success for it to feed on. The easiest game Failure has found to keep you always providing dinner is to get you into a game of **'Almost.'**

The Game of 'Almost'

Are any of these familiar to you or someone you care about?

> "Aww, you almost got that job, too bad. You should have done your homework instead of goofing off all the time. You'll likely never get a good job with that amount of education."
>
> "Geez ... you almost got a date with that great looking guy but maybe next time."
>
> "Oops, you lost all your money in that business and you were so close to making it. Yes, you knew that big deal would go south but you went ahead anyway. Maybe you are the loser you keep telling yourself in your mind."
>
> "Wow... you got 5 A's on your report card but oh boy that B was a big letdown. How come daddy was so mad? Maybe you're not as smart as you think you are."
>
> "Darn... and you almost got off the booze that time, but wasn't that a helluva party? How come that pretty girl didn't fall down laughing like everyone else when you danced 'the monster mash' walking down the bar? You know, I found out that she was really attracted to you but her father was a drunk so she won't go out with guys who drink. But that babe in the corner passed out, she looks like she'd spend some time with you."
>
> "Vegetables smegetables... I know I told you that there's never calories in ice cream if you have it on Thursdays, but I was just foolin' with ya. And now you've gone and given yourself cancer. You dumb bugger, you might as well quit this place now."

"Wow, wait my friend... don't pull the trigger. You might not be worth much but you are all we have. Think of your son, you can't just abandon him. You'll be able to give him what you've always dreamed of soon, just as soon as you get your mojo back. Now give me the gun buddy. I'll hold it for you in case you ever need it again."

"Man look at you go boy. You've made it all the way to being President of the United States and that intern... yee haw, did that dolly know how to kiss or what and you should have seen the energy come off you when you brought out that cigar. I know you promised yourself you'd never do it again, that you loved your wife that much, and you almost made it brother. Guilt sex is the best isn't it, no doubt about it."

"Damn it sister... don't you know you are too fat, too old and too dumb, and you almost got a date because he likes you but then you got sick from all that cheesecake. Don't worry honey, I'll just lie with you a bit while you feed that shame you have buried beneath that cute little fat body of yours."

Failure thrives in the games of **Almost, Coulda, Woulda, Shoulda, Too Busy, Better Over There, Try Again. and More.** (Try Again is not the same as hope because in Try Again you do the same thing over again but double down this time with energy and bravado. It doesn't work all the time but Failure really enjoys watching you spin your tires). You play along and for some reason never remember the ending no matter how many times you've played each game.

You keep listening but for some reason can't make out the voices and what they are saying. Failure says too much of Nothing and Success says, "Over here my friend, Everything is waiting for you." We do get a glimpse of it accidentally every once in a while, at the edge of our dreams, or when the light is just right. Success and Failure live with other ideas just above the spectrum of light that humans can see. .(See Ledwith on Orbs)

http://hiddenlighthouse.wordpress.com/tag/dr-miceal-ledwith

So we play this game of Failure and Success with ourselves and we finance the whole deal. We give our energy to both. If we fed Success more than Failure it would run out of steam and probably go away but we'd have to be 'awake' and aware to do that. You get to choose who you play with because you're paying all the bills. When do you plan to get around to switching partners? The first step is to make a list of all the things Failure has said to you over the years when you got drawn into a game of Almost. The longer the list the easier Failure is to see.

(Stop right now and answer this question. Exactly what time in the next 24 hours is the time when you are going to sit down and put some energy and focus into making this list? Write down a time and then make it non-negotiable no matter how much it looks and feels like you should do something else or someone just 'pops in' for a visit at that exact time.)

> **Worthiness Principle - There is a very real part inside us that is committed to us failing at Success and succeeding at Failure and we need to pay attention to it so doesn't have its way with us much longer.**

Receiving Is The Greatest Giving of All

Our culture gives almost a 100 percent of its attention on learning how *to 'Go out and Get.'* I think it's because we're all too damn busy *"mistaking activity for accomplishment"* as Zig Ziglar used to say.

As 'feeling superior' is allowed and even encouraged in our culture **"it is better to give than to receive"** allows us to feel worthy 'out there' while 'allowing ourselves to Receive' is proof that we actually know that we are worthy.

Achievement More And Then More Again

All of us, when we are breaking away from being a dependent on our parents and community, need to call loudly in our culture, *"Go out and get him hotshot. You can do it! Go for it!"*

Get an education, a job, a soul mate, a car, a house, two cars, kids, more kids, one big car, money, savings, security, wealth, achievement, success, respect. This is the path we all seem so wildly enthusiastic about as evidenced by the two-hour traffic gridlock on the Los Angeles freeway every single day.

The more we get out there in the spirit of getting, the harder we try and the more we push, the more cheering we hear from our fans. Many people achieve a lot from multi-tasking 23 hours a day. But it is a law of the Universe that for all the energy that we put out there, energy in some form will come back to us multiplied, rewarding us for all the work we've done... unless we're busy out working when it is delivered or we don't realize that things have fundamentally changed and we are now in the land of Receiving. Instead, most people figure: 'if 'going out and getting' earns that much applause then doubling it will just blow the applause through the roof.'

Not so fast all you Donald Trump fans; there comes a time when the next lesson *is 'learning how to receive'* the benefits. But we usually push it aside because we're too busy working our ass off paying the bills and the loan interest we owe from giving away so much of our future as a result of buying our 5,000 square foot house, (in which we use less than 1,000 to live in most of the time).

One obvious reason why we don't get the hint when it's time to Receive is that we've sold too much of our future to trust that enough Receiving will come in to support our lifestyle. But that also implies that you are Receiving at the same time as you're getting, whereas true Receiving comes to you without notice and lies quietly at your feet waiting for you to sit down, relax and notice.

The other main reason is that we think we are being gracious and humble by not accepting that which is coming to us. Even here we have the wrong idea. It's not gracious to put aside a gift from Receiving, it is disrespectful at its core. We are saying, in effect, that we don't need what is being offered and that which offered it, and at the same time they aren't smart enough to choose something we do want. None of this is Receiving because it assumes you are Receiving now for something that you gave. True Receiving is allowing and absorbing without restriction or hesitation all of the love, joy and connection that is contained in what you are receiving, which is coming to you for no reason except because you are you.

When we first rounded the corner into the land of Receiving we are unskilled. Allow Receiving without hesitation will produce emotional heat for awhile as we gently move aside all the guilt and shame that we allowed to accumulate throughout our life. We have to suspend, if only for a short while, all the mistaken beliefs and judgments we have pinned on ourselves in preparation for our crucifixion.

In short we need only suspend the argument we've been having with ourselves and accept the truth once and for all... that we are enough. We are enough, we always were enough and we always will be without a single drop of effort being expended. Our unworthiness begins to melt away and Receiving will shortly follow.

Here is an excellent article written by Karen Mead on the blog Tiny Buddha: Simple Wisdom for Complex Lives: Learning To Receive: 5

Steps To Opening Up

(Now for all you atheists out there don't get the idea you have to adopt some of that booga booga spiritual stuff in order to be able to Receive. The only thing you really need to Receive is willingness and sincerity. If you can't muster those up you might as well sit down and relax. You're going to be here for a while.)

Connection to 'Everything' is our only Desire

It seems to us we live in two worlds, the one outside of our head and the one inside. What is more accurate is that everything is going on inside our head. What you see outside can only be interpreted on the inside, and the opposite is not true. Looking at our reflection of ourselves in a mirror we are aware that 'we' are out there but we know that the only one who can answer back is the one inside.

You might get praised for being on time for work but that praise which comes from 'out there' is only a reflection of the choices and decisions we made inside. No matter what you are doing or where you are doing it or what is happening it is all happing inside your mind. But the mind is a big place from which to operate. It seems boundary- less. So how do you ever know where you are?

> "We must be willing to let go of the life we planned so as to have the life that is waiting for us."
>
> ~ Joseph Campbell

What Impacts Your Worthiness Quotient

Things that Affects Your Worthiness Quotient

The answer is everything that you have ever said, not said, done, not done, thought, believed, let go of, not let go of and kept a secret.

While accurate, knowing that, 'everything', is not very helpful because you can't do anything about the past and you don't have all the knowledge, skills and awareness to sufficiently impact the present. Each and everyone one will cause you to turn towards Everything or Nothing and determine the speed at which you go there. In no particular order here are some of the hundreds of things that affect your WSP and WQ:

- Public Profile versus Private Profile.
- The difference between the Truth and the version that you tell.
- Your willingness and ability to allow a new truth to emerge.
- The good/bad things you have done versus the good/bad things you think you have done.
- Your Universal Bank Account
- Inner / Outer World Conversations with yourself.
- Your willingness to not play the Shoulda, Coulda, Woulda game
- An awareness of your subjective nature.
- You commitment to be the objective Observer in the face of the judgments we have against ourselves.
- The judgments we think others have against us.
- Your awareness of self punishment you are inflicting upon yourself and encouraging others to inflict as well.

Outer versus Inner World Persona

We all have a public persona that we show the world and a personal persona that we keep to ourselves.

People don't think of you as a thief yet you know you used to steal things out of coats when you were a coat check girl. Secretly one of the judgments you have on yourself is that you are a thief.

People think you have a lot of money but you know you owe way more than you have. Secretly you believe yourself to be a loser and one who lies. You've projected out into the world that you are smart but you know you make mistakes every day and that you made some biggies in the past.

You invest time, money and effort to show the world that you are a nice person yet you've bullied your wife, children and co-workers many times, and it began in the sandbox with the other kids. Secretly you've known for a long time that you are not very nice and are not a very good person at all.

All of these kinds of judgments you have against yourself are going to affect your Setpoint and Quotient. It takes some reflection and brute honesty to come to the awareness of judgments like this. We all have our favorites and then we have ones we wouldn't admit no matter how much someone tortured us. The thing to realize is that someone is already torturing you and they are brutal... they are you.

Use the Life Balance Wheel at the beginning of the book to make a list of judgments you have against yourself. You don't have to write down all the details but there are no degrees of guilt. You are either guilty or not. You are not guilty but it takes some work to come to that conclusion.

Your Universal Bank Account

As all things in life are about Relationship it is useful to view your transactions with all living things, (man, animal, fish, plant, the earth), as being a like a bank account.

In the relationship, nice things are done by you and the other person (deposit). Sometimes we make mistakes, (withdrawals), and sometime we forgive, (deposit), and sometimes we do harm deliberately, (withdrawal). Every transaction that serves the safety and well being of yourself and others builds up a positive balance in your account. Both parties make deposits.

Sometimes we screw up and make a withdrawal but because the relationship has a positive balance the consequences are not all that great. If one or both parties go into NEEDS and start making withdrawals then sooner or later they're going to be in Overdraft. Both people can save the account from being closed but if one feels they need to make a lot of deposits, and the other person feels they have been wronged by the depositor and makes withdrawals faster than the other can make deposits, then the relationship will end and be dissolved. We might forget or cover over the discrepancies in the account and hold the judgment at a level that keeps it from our every day awareness, but our body never does. Kinesiology will help you find these issues.

Our Perceptions of What Happened

Take any four people standing on each of the four corners of an intersection, waiting to cross the street, plus four more who are back several feet from the Intersection.

There is a car accident at the Intersection. Two cars collide and then speed off.

You are a journalist and you interview all eight people. Which car hit the other first? How fast was each car going? Was the driver of each car a man or a woman? Who is to blame for the accident? What color were the cars?

How many people agree with each other about what happened?

None of them. Everybody has a different perspective. Everyone sees things differently. Everyone, if they don't get talked out of it, believes that their perspective is the correct one so it's not what actually happened but it's what we 'believe' happened. Everyone's mind was in a different state at the time of the accident. Some people were awake, some tired, some going over a fight they have had with someone either recently or years ago.

The minute the accident happened our ego wakes us up to what is going on around us. 'Am I safe?' is the first question, but there are several more that happened in a millisecond.

- Do I need to fight, flight or do nothing, (freeze), in this situation in order to get safe?
- Based upon past experiences what is likely to happen next?
- Based upon the past what should I do about it?
- Are there any other dangers? (Pickpockets love accidents.)

Our perspective is based upon what we see, observe, think, feel, believe and know what happened.

No matter what really happened our perspective will be based upon our version of the past because - just as we decided on what happened now, (which is not accurate simply because of our physical location), we also made decisions that were not, and are not, accurate about the events that happened in our past. The feeling this accident evokes in us is based upon a memory of the past.

Six months later the incident goes to trial. Each of the people you interviewed is called as a witness and each tells a modified version of what they saw happen. Sometimes their current version is radically different from the version you recorded at the scene. Why?

In the six months that followed they repeated the incident many times in their mind to determine if they were actually safe or not and they also repeated the story to others. The version that they repeated to others, is not based upon what happened but on what they believe to have happened, based upon what they now 'know' about what happens 'in these kinds of things.'

- If their father was a lousy driver there is a better chance that you will see each car was driven recklessly, by a man. If your mother forbade you from taking the car for a drive for some reason, when you really wanted to go for a drive, then the drivers are more likely to be women.
- If mother and father fought a lot in the car or even anywhere else the story is more likely to be that there was a man and woman driving the cars that crashed.
- If your younger brother used to taunt you in the back seat and always got you in trouble then the story is likely to be that the drivers were younger.
- If a friend died in a car crash it could be that the traffic lights were to blame.

The mind makes up stories to connect the dots and make sense of things so we will be safe in the future. We remember things not as they actually happened but according to what we believe 'was likely to have happened' based upon what happened to us in the past.

Subjective Versus Objective

No one, I mean *'no one'* is objective. We are all subjective about what did happen, what's happening now and what will happen. Not even the Dali Lama is objective because he knows that it is karma and that you will come back again to learn the lessons you were supposed to learn in this situation and didn't.

The Past Is Never Really The Past

The past is what we decided it was. We make the whole thing up. Nevertheless our current Worthiness Setpoint and Quotient is based upon what we feel and believe what we and everyone else Shoulda, Coulda, Woulda done to make the whole situation safer.

For example:

- The past will determine the insurance settlement you ask for and will allow yourself to receive arising from any accident you are in.
- It will affect the settlement others get based on the difference between your conduct in public versus how 'guilty' you considered yourself in a situation similar.
- It will affect the degree of compassion you will show to people and to yourself in any similar situation or any situation that reminds you of the current situation.
- It will determine whether you give or take more energy from the situation. It will determine what the current balance is in your Universal Bank Account.

The lyrics from the Elton John song "Circle of Life" give us many of the reasons that affect our ability to receive all of what life has to offer:

From the day we arrive on the planet
And blinking, step into the sun
There's more to be seen than can ever be seen
More to do than can ever be done Some say eat or be eaten Some say live and let live But all are agreed as they join the stampede You should never take more than you give in the circle of life

Some of us fall by the wayside And some of us soar to the stars
And some of us sail through our troubles
And some have to live with the scars.

Fear Causes Change of Direction

Fear is the basic reason why we change direction and head back into "How Bad Will I Let It Get?" territory. There are two popular acronyms for Fear:

1. Forget Everything And Run
2. False Evidence Appearing Real

We experience FEAR so early in life. Our Worthiness Setpoint is established unconsciously by false premise. As a result we end up living a common life, far below our potential. We make a simple mistake that has profound consequences:

> "Based upon false evidence appearing real we forget Everything and accidently run away from our innate innocence and immeasurable value."

The choice we would have made if we had the awareness at the time would have been to make FEAR our friend and use it to excite us instead of cause us to Fight, Flight or Freeze you

To do this we must choose to look at FEAR from completely the opposite direction. FEAR then becomes:

Face Everything and Rise

You have this choice each and every second of your entire life. Commit to using this definition each and every time instead and life become much more of an adventure.

What You Feed Expands

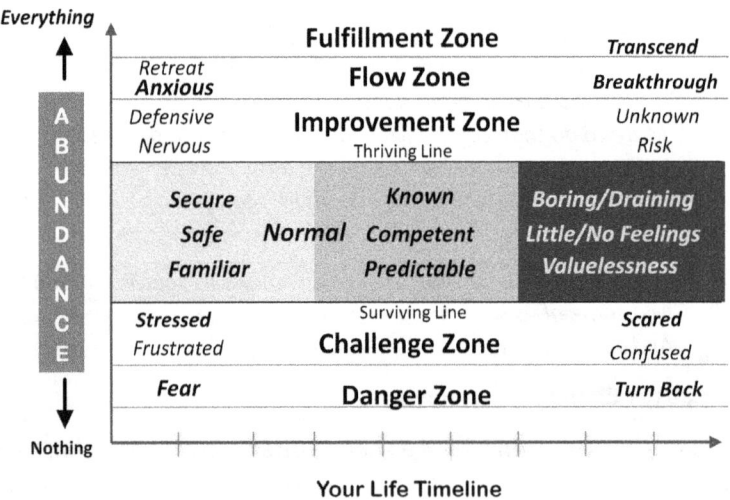

Feelings provide the clue as to where we are in our Cycle and therefore give us a chance to decide whether to keep going in a certain direction or stop and change direction. While there are feelings that are painful on both sides of our WSP they are different types of

feelings. As we rise we are more likely to be feeling anxious thoughts and on the down side we are more likely to be feeling Fear type thoughts.

Our Setpoint and Quotient are based upon what we focus on. In this section I have explained why our WSP and WQ are affected to the negative and almost no time talking about how to 'increase' them.

Be Aware The Soft Voice

Be discerning of the soft voice that says 'just one more'

- just one more cocktail
- just one more cookie
- just one more mile on a long trip that has your eyes drooping into sleep
- just one more kiss with your secretary
- you should do it... you know you're a good person, you deserve it, you're entitled to it.
- just one more shoot 'em up show

Any time you hear a voice in your head where you don't know whether it is your actual intuition speaking to you, is a time for you to stab yourself in your leg with a fork and wake up from the trance that you've falling into. (Well, skip the fork thing but at least give yourself a pinch or snap your fingers to interrupt the thoughts that are coming from your old buddy who says he loves you but has never actually come through with anything except pain and suffering).

> *"Beliefs have the power to create and the power to destroy. Human beings have the awesome ability to take any experience of their lives and create a meaning that disempowers them or one that can literally save their lives."*
>
> ~ Tony Robbins

The Way Back to Abundance

Feelings Tell You Where You Are

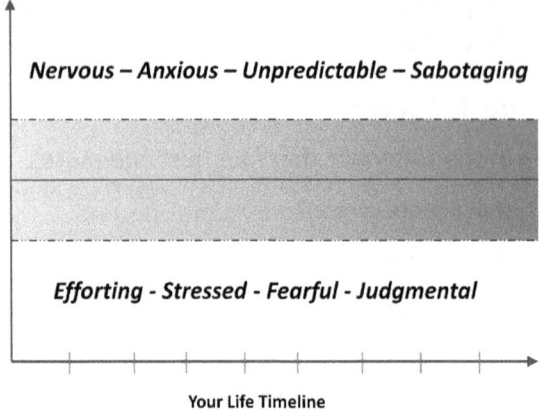

15 Ways to Gain Access to Worthiness

1. Give up your need to always be right.
2. Give up your need for control.
3. Give up on Blame and Shame
4. Give up your self-defeating self-talk.
5. Give up your limiting beliefs
6. Give up complaining
7. Give up the luxury of criticism
8. Give up your need to impress others
9. Give up your resistance to change
10. Give up labels
11. Give up your fears
12. Give up excuses
13. Give up the past
14. Give up Attachment
15. Give up living your life to other's expectations

Our Feelings Tell Us Where We Are
Letting Go and Unlearning

Yes, it is that simple. There are just a few small things to let go of that have been holding you back from rising to *Everything*. Unhooking from any and all of the beliefs you have that result in thoughts that cause you to show up in the world with:

(From Power Versus Force by David R. Hawkins)

- Anything you insist on being right about...
- Anything that you are not willing to let go of
- Anything you are not willing to un-learn
- Yes, Everything wants to live forever but it is your choice how much you feed the habits, ideas, and attitudes that are not in our highest truth.

"I am bigger than anything that can happen to me. All these things, sorrow, misfortune, and suffering, are outside my door. I am in the house and I have the key."

~ Charles Fletcher Lummis

How long is all this going to take?

Yes, it seems like a lot but it's not nearly as hard as it might seem.

- Some of these beliefs, thoughts and Judgments you have already made it through.
- Some of them you're almost through, that taking one step 'in faith' and you're free.
- The Awareness that you have gained from this book will lift you quickly through several more.
- Some will happen naturally as a result of living.
- Some will evaporate as result of others who have made it through those already.
- With some you will be helped by someone you love. Your enemies will pull you through others.
- Some you will let go of as a result of Higher Mind practices like Mediations and Mindfulness.
- Others will be being carried along with a crowd.
- Some leave as a result of dysfunctions that cause others pain.

- Some beliefs, thoughts and judgments you will get beyond as a result of helping others directly.
- Others will just leave because you loved all the rest.
- Some will be carried along with others that you let go of.
- Others will escape as a result of someone prying open the heavily locked door of your heart.
- Some you will let go of because you made a Choice and gave that choice enough energy to allow it to happen with ease.
- Some you will sword fight with for a minute, or a lifetime.
- Everyone of us has made it through many and have that to offer you as you have the gift of freedom for others.
- This is what Ram Dass meant when he said 'We're all just walking each other home."

> "Once you make a decision, the universe conspires to make it happen."
>
> ~ Ralph Waldo Emerson

The Fastest Way to 'Everything'

First of all why did we end up with all this baggage that weighs us down? *'We didn't think it was funny!'*

That's it. Instead of making light of it we took whatever was happening seriously. A Course In Miracles says it the best: "You are here because you forgot to laugh." The minute we allow ourselves to take something personally and we start to suspect that we might be guilty is the moment it gets hold of you.

> *"If you're going to be able to look back at something and laugh about it, you might as well laugh about it now."*
>
> ~ Marie Osmond

Have you sinned or made mistake?

If you have the eyes to see and the courage to see, you will see that you have done every one of these things to others and yourself. If you spend some mind time on it you can probably describe several other ways not listed here that you employed to save you from Success, Joy and Love.

This is all a huge mistake and if you were watching it played out on television... I'd bet that other than the things that have happened to you in real life you would find the whole thing hilarious.

How many times have you had your friends rolling on the floor in laughter as you told them a story about where you had screwed up and still don't think it's funny... getting so drunk at a wedding that you lost the ring you were supposed to hand to your best friend the groom, who still isn't speaking to you; running over the neighbors' dog when you were backing out of the driveway... having a fight with your son that was so intense you were smashing furniture over each other like in a spaghetti western, (my friend also had that happen to him)?

All of these are just mistakes. If you had had an awareness of the Worthiness Cycle, most if not all of these things would have been averted or would have been much less intense.

You can't be guilty of something if you didn't know what it actually was. And to do so is 'indulgence' which is an easy and convenient way to save us from Abundance.

If you knew the path that made up your father's Worthiness Setpoint you wouldn't be feeling irreparably damaged... you would be feeling nothing but compassion.

If you knew what was really going on when you ran away from the person that loved you the most you wouldn't be beating yourself up so much by acting undeserving of love.

If you really knew why your father, wife or brother was drowning in the booze that was killing them you would be able to 'let go and let God handle it' because you knew at the deepest part of you that you are Innocent and have infinite value and so does everyone else.

"Addictions are the stuff that Less is made of."

~ Allan Hunkin

Transforming into Good

Every culture and tradition describes something that we would call 'the process of Forgiveness' The process of forgiveness is simply the process of recognizing that this is all just a huge mistake and everyone involved played a part in an unspoken agreement to use something to hold us all back from being Everything.

We played our part, the other person played their part... everyone was in on the act and everyone learned something that they needed to learn to get past one or more of the beliefs that we use as a buffer between us and Unconditional Love.

If you had the courage you'd invite them all over to your house for a barbeque and laugh about it all hilariously until the sun came up. What forgiveness is really, beyond the Hollywood and Religions versions of it, is you coming to the awareness that it was all a mistake, you wanted to be right about something, forgot to laugh and insisted on the other person not laughing as well.

An 'In Person' Forgiveness Scenario

There are many books written about the process of forgiveness but here's a simple, step by step process.

First you get the person's undivided attention. Then center yourself in your own Innocence and you say:

"I'm sorry for what happened... as of this moment I will no longer allow this to be between us and protect us from all the love, peace and joy of Abundance.

You ask the person if they have heard you. If they say yes, break out the bubbly... if they say no or you sense that they are unsure, you say it exactly the same way and you add something like this:

And this is the last time I will ever apologize for this because to do more would be to you hold you and myself guilty for what was a mistake and a misunderstanding of what we were both going through.

If we had known any better way at the time to try to make it through life we would have never played it out the way we did. Let's move on. Your Innocence is far more important to me than this story we have held each other prisoner to.

I love you and that's the only thing that matters. I'm going to join the others now who are having fun in the kitchen. Please join me when you've had a moment to soak in what I have just said and the gift I have given us both today."

And with that you're done. The rest is the distance they must travel to retrieve the reality of their own Innocence. You cannot do it for them and if you try you will be robbing them of territory that they have to become aware of to gain an understanding and therefore the gift of Abundance that's waiting for them.

There is one more step that you do after you've done the one above. Sit quietly somewhere peaceful and after a moment to center yourself you say out loud or in your mind, it doesn't matter:

"I forgive myself for believing that I was wrong, guilty or inadequate"

"In this situation. I simple made a mistake in identity and got some bad advice from a voice in my head which I now understand does not have my best intentions at heart. I know I need do nothing to attain my Innocence for it never left me. This is the last time I will forgive myself for believing these things because to take one more second to indulge myself is another second I am holding myself back on my journey to Everything.

Hallelujah, Praise be to God, Allah and Bill Gates... I'm hungry for food, grins and giggles. Amen.

That's pretty much the show folks. After that it's off to new and unknown territory which will be filled with the good, the bad, the ugly and... the beautiful (everybody forgets that one) anxiety and fear but no worries as the Aussies say, "No worries... it's all good mate." Eventually you will realize that the Fears, no matter how intense, are a production of the part of your mind that doesn't want you to succeed. Life really starts to get interesting... ask Jesus about it the next time you talk.

Be Out Ahead

In making Worthiness work for you, you must have 'tools' in place ahead of time to make sure you come out ahead without allowing your own lack of awareness take you out of the game, in any given situation. The formula to make that happen is **Awareness, Commitment and Action,** awareness, commitment and action. Did I mention awareness, commitment and action?

Awareness

What's about to happen... what is happening, really and what just happened? With so much coming at us in this crazy sped-up world it is really easy to get lulled to sleep. It's embarrassing to admit that most of us are sleepwalking through life, but in fact we are. Most of us are fully enveloped in at least three interloping trances at the same time. (see 'Trance: From Magic to Technology' by Dennis R. Wier)

With so many facets pushing to have more market share of your mind, it would be impossible to remain out of a trance. The media, the news channels, the entertainment industry, the political class, the education and intellectual classes, the business, entrepreneurial and capitalist class, the environmental, governmental, and third world class... all these are competing for your time and attention. You need to know that it is almost impossible that you have not been lulled into a walking sleep and have therefore have become part of the walking dead.

Just accept it and you'll wake up a lot easier than if you try to deny it. If It's any easier you need to know that I have walked through a lot of my life. I have squandered my natural innate talents and I have found myself waking up in the middle of the perpetration of a crime, (not legal but emotional), and the only words that made any sense were 'how the hell did I get here... again?'

Commitment

Once you reach the stage in life where you are making all your own decisions, there a lot of things to think about. At first we are thinking about everything all at once but as soon as we decide who we are going to marry, and then do marry them, you don't have to think about those things again and the load in our mind gets lighter, which gives you more access to Worthiness.

As soon as you decide your occupation and begin to go about the process of mastering it, you don't have to think about that and you gain more access to Worthiness.

Once you decide to go about rising above your limiting beliefs you don't have to think about whether you are going in that direction which makes the process of actually doing it much more efficient and fun.

The part of us that doesn't want us to succeed is going to wake up a friend of theirs by the name of *'Rebel'*, and the two of them are going to gang up on you and try to convince you that Commitment is Bondage and Servitude. They are going to tell you that it's scary and it is pulling you towards Nothing. And they are not going to do this just once. They are going to do it every single time you gain the opportunity to establish a higher Worthiness Setpoint.

This is not the end of this conspiracy. The higher you rise toward *Everything* the more sophisticated they get and more convincing they become. They are no longer shouting in your ear by this point but rather they are whispering to you like a good friend. If they sense a speck of fear or loneliness they will move in and it will take you years and a lot of unnecessary effort to evict them.

The real truth is that Commitment is Freedom and always makes you lighter and therefore lifts you towards your next level of Worthiness.

Commit to your own well-being and you have taken a quantum leap in Freedom. Make a commitment to rise to new heights.

Write it down, and then write it down again and again until you have it firmly imprinted in your mind. Write down the parts of your commitment that are non-negotiable. Tell at least three people what your commitment is and have them remind you if they see you straying from your commitment.

Review your commitment at least once a month so that you won't have to review it when you're up against something that is trying to get you to break your commitment.

A Deal is a Deal

One of my clients once who told me a story I'll never forget.

John had been a member of a heavy metal rock band in the late 1970s. He said drugs were always around but he never paid too much attention to them. He used drugs but he wasn't wide-eyed fascinated like others in the band.

Soon the band was touring and one day John made a commitment to himself that if drugs were to ever get hold of him he would quit them on the spot and never touch drugs again.

About ten years later John woke up in a hotel room. He had been using cocaine for almost two weeks nonstop.

When he got out of bed he looked in the mirror and he literally did not recognize the guy that was looking back at him. He said it took him a couple of minutes to realize that the image was of him and he realized in that moment that cocaine had gotten him.

John took a shower, got dressed and walked out of that hotel and never touched cocaine or any other drug or alcohol ever again.

I said *"You just quit, no rehab, no counseling or help from anyone? You just quit one of the most addicting substances on the planet and you did it without any help whatsoever?"*

"Yes" he replied.

After all the people I had worked with who had a terrible time getting off that drug I asked *"How did you do it?"*

"A deal is a deal Allan, a deal is a deal."

All I could do was look away. *"Wow,"* I said, *"I wish I had that kind of conviction and character."*

What is non-negotiable for you?

Where is it that you are going to make your stand? When you find it you'll find Worthiness makes its home there as well.

Action

Worthiness work is pretty 'heady.' It's easy to get stuck in our heads and let everything swirl around without us actually doing anything. Worthiness rises with action. Get moving now!

Get Out Of The Details

One of the easiest ways that our EMaEo takes us out is by getting us to think that we need all the facts before making a decision and getting into action. Asking everyone's opinion is just another way to avoid acting. The details affect Flow, every solution comes first from the abstract. Insisting on getting into the details is a camouflage for Perfection, which will hold you back from upping your worthiness quotient as much as anything.

An excellent resource for getting out of details is a book by Dr. Steven Hays entitled "Get Out of Your Mind and Into Your Life: The New Acceptance and Commitment."

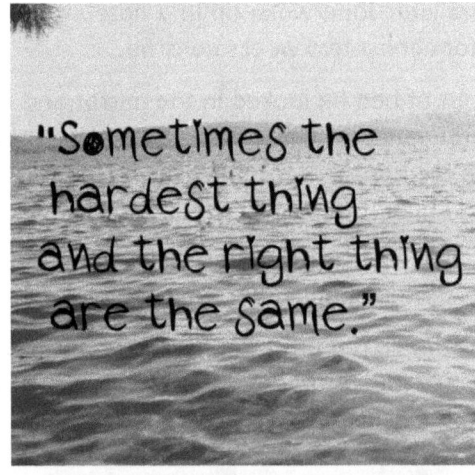

Upping Your Worthiness Quotient

Things I Overheard While Out Walking With Myself

What do you say when you talk to yourself and how many times does each word or phrase echo back to you in a given hour, day, week, year?

I don't know exactly what you say to yourself when you are awake or asleep but it is easy to tell what you say because all anyone has to do is look at how your life is working and they will know what your self-talk consists of. It takes a long time to realize that what you say to yourself has a direct cause and effect. If you want to change your level of worthiness you only have to look closely at your self-talk and decide which is healthy and leading you towards abundance and which is not.

Words Tell Us The Thoughts We Are Thinking.

Plot this out on a piece of paper and start jotting down words and phrases that come out of your mouth (mind).

Word / Thought Direction   **Positive**   **Negative**

Things you say to yourself

Things you say about yourself

Things you say to others

Things you say about others

Things you say to 'the World / Universe'

Things you say about 'the World / Universe'

Now, take a close look at each of the words and phrases and ask yourself the following questions:

- Is that word or phrase true about myself, others or the world?
- Is that word or phrase helpful in my quest for more Success, Happiness and Fulfillment?
- What word/phrase could I use instead?
- How am I going to remember to say those words first?

Finding Your Trigger Points

Let us review some of the principles outlined in this book:

- Worthiness and our ability to Receive is so close to our being that it is mostly invisible.
- The influence it has on each transaction we have with ourselves and others is more than we are aware of.
- There is a part of our mind that has grown over time into a type of mind virus and now has its own agenda.
- This part of your mind needs for you to almost succeed and then not, because it feeds on the negative energy that comes from fear, frustration, disappointment and failure.

If you succeed it doesn't get to feed on the negative energy and it loses power. Eventually, if you have many successes in a row it doesn't have enough power to stay invisible and you get to see it for what it is, and you are able to counter its influence to the point where it just goes to sleep. You then have an almost un-restricted path to Everything.

- In trying to keep power its voice is soft and subtle and it wins at having you changing direction and heading back down to Nothing without even noticing.
- This part of our mind wants to us to succeed at failing.
- Without awareness and action that part of our mind will occupy, take over and have too much influence over how we act and react.
- We must be constantly aware, and vigilant, in noticing "Am I heading up towards *Everything* or down towards Nothing in this current situation and in this current moment within this situation?"
- We can and do switch in direction in a millisecond.
- Everyone has an overall Worthiness, and then we have our year, month and day-long time frames where you can go up and down through the whole cycle in one day, even one minute.
- The key to returning to an upward movement is to notice quickly when you have come in contact with one of your fears and have changed direction.
- We can switch several times in the course of a conversation

'Trigger Points' is a term used in Emotional Intelligence literature. There are lots of resources available on the Internet.

(Joe Wilner Shake Off the Grind: How Do You Trigger Positive? Find Your Pathways to Happiness)

When exploring your triggers break them down into two types.

External triggers - These are anything that happens in the environment. This can come from emotional events and life circumstances, or what someone says or does to you.

Internal triggers - These are what we tell ourselves about the external triggers. It's our internal dialogue and thinking process making interpretations about the external trigger. As Hans Selye says, "It's not stress that kills us, it is our reaction to it."

This from Byron Stock's Emotional Intelligence Blog: Identifying Your Emotional.

Emotional Self-Awareness is the foundational competency of Emotional Intelligence. Emotional Self-Awareness is being aware of "what" your feelings are; not "how" you are feeling. Identifying people, things and events that trigger your emotions (whether positive or negative) is a first step to becoming emotionally self-aware. Following the simple steps below will help you identify your emotional triggers and enable you to think more clearly during emotionally charged situations.

The first step is to understand that you are responding to the primal "fight or flight" reaction when you are faced with a physical or psychological threat. It's easy to see that negative emotions can result from physical threats, but there are also psychological threats that can trigger negative emotions.

Psychological threats include being frustrated in pursuing a goal, being treated unjustly, being demeaned or insulted, as well as having your dignity/self-esteem or security threatened.

Thousands of years ago our emotional triggers were more likely comprised of physical threats - our daily goal was to survive predators, famine and whatever else the day brought. Today our hot buttons are typically psychological threats.

Next, identify and list those people, events, situations or things that evoke negative emotions, (anger, annoyance, hurt, frustration, etc.). Some of these you will be able to recall, others you might list as you go through your day or week. For example:

- when someone cuts you off while you are making a point.
- when you are about to make a difficult phone call.
- when you find yourself annoyed just by seeing an email has arrived from someone.
- when your teenager comes home with a 'D' on a paper
- when you don't have the resources required to finish a project you are responsible for
- when you hear that the company is going to reorganize again
- when a project deadline is shortened dramatically
- when a parent is ill and you need to make arrangements to care for him or her
- when you show up to a meeting on time and only half the people are there
- when you see a family member who causes contention in the family
- you keep getting interrupted while trying to meet a deadline.

Finally, look over your list and identify those hot buttons, (people, things, situations), that evoke the strongest negative emotions. It may not be possible to avoid these, but just being alerted to how emotionally charged these situations can be can help you to start managing the negative emotions and think more clearly under pressure. This knowledge can help you have a better, more productive experience.

Awareness of the principles of Worthiness Cycle is gained by asking a few questions several times a day:

> *"Am I running towards something I think I need or am I running away from something that I think has me triggered?"*

Time Link

Sometimes we've turned around and are running away from something that is actually very good for us but we think is too much for us to handle. We need to remember this when we need to remember this.

What time is it now? Look at your watch! Put your index finger from your hand on the clock face and leave it there. Now ask one or more questions that will wake you up.

Linking a *'Worthiness Check In'* to every time we check the time helps us to remember to check in and see what is going on several times a day. It doesn't matter whether it is a clock in the kitchen, on the DVD player, on our wrist, on our wake-up alarm clock, or in the town square, (stop and go back and read this list, stopping to picture each one separately in your mind).

Remember to Ask Yourself Questions

Ask yourself at least three of the questions listed here. Why three? Because your *eMaEo* will have erected a wall to stop you from gaining a full understanding. Asking three questions in a row will get you past one or more of the walls.

- Am I in "How Good Can I Stand It?" or "How Bad Will I Let It Get?"
- Which direction am I currently heading: Up to Abundance or Down to Nothing?
- What caused me to change direction?
- What will it take for me to change now and head up even faster to Abundance?
- What am I needing to be right about here that if I just let go of the need to be right I would return to Ease and Flow?

Hello eMaEo

Hello eMaEo... What are you saying to me right now that both you and I know is not in my best interests, nor yours either?

Hello eMaEo... What do you see ahead of us, that I don't see yet, that is going to lead us to Nothing?

Hello eMaEo... Are you having fun with me and I need to laugh so I can get back on track?

A Good Friend of Yours

Ask yourself "If I was a good friend of mine, who always was honest with me, what would I be saying to me right now about my current level of Worthiness and the direction I'm heading?"

"Why am I creating this NOW?"

Look at your watch, then look up and ask out loud the following questions:

"**WHY** am I creating this now?"

"Why **am 'I'** (you specifically) creating this now?"

"Why am I **CREATING** this now?"

"Why am I creating **THIS** now?"

"Why am I creating this **NOW**?"

" Nothing ever goes away until it teaches us we what need to now."

~ Pema Chödrön

Measurement Doesn't Exist In 'Everything'

As you up your Worthiness Quotient you will at some point begin to naturally develop your Spiritual Quotient. At the junction of the two are some choices you have to make to be able to receive and absorb the next level of Abundance on your way to *Everything*.

There are some things you can't be a little bit of...one is pregnant... you either are or you aren't.

You either choose your Innocence or allow degrees of shame, guilt and fear.

You either choose to see the total Innocence of all mankind or allow yourself to believe that at our core, mankind is Evil.

You either choose to know there is a Heaven or you allow yourself to believe in Sin, Hell and Damnation.

You either choose to be in Empathy knowing that this is all part of an ever-changing path back to Connection and Everything or you allow yourself to believe that in the end this is all pointless and Nothing.

You can't be 99.9999% Innocent and you can't believe that anyone and everyone is 0.00001% Guilty.

Upward And Onward

Somehow, your Intuition was loud enough to get you to read this book. In so doing, it knew something you previously only suspected. You were ready for the journey toward ever expanding abundance.

Now that you have finished reading this book, you are at choice. When you find yourself racing towards nothing, you can choose to alter the course of your life, look the greatest fear in the human mind straight in the eye, stop yourself from running away from having it all, turn around, and head directly back towards your birthright: your innocence and true value.

Every single person on the planet, since the beginning of time, was, is, and always will be innocent and worthy of everything they desire. The journey is simply to rediscover the truth of our original innocence and innate value.

You now have awareness of this inalterable Truth: Worthiness is everyone's innate birthright, and therefore the fundamental principle of integrity.

You're on your way!

I am writing the conclusion to this book a few days before my sixtieth birthday. The ups and downs I have cycled through in my life's journey have been rapid, intense and challenging. In retrospect I know that my life would have been much less challenging if I had paid more attention to the teachings that came my way.

It has taken almost a life time for me to realize that accepting my innate Worth is the single most valuable gift I have ever allowed myself to receive.

Accepting your profound value and worth is the most significant contribution you will make to the world and to everyone you love.

I can say without hesitation that understanding and implementing the principles presented herein will be as empowering and transformational for you as they have been for me and even more.

Don't be embarrassed if you feel, at this point, that you haven't understood the workings of the Worthiness Cycle just yet. It takes a while. There is no rush because to rush through this is to rush through life itself. Trust that the Mind never forgets.

Being the mindful Observer of your life provides Awareness. Combining ever evolving Awareness with Worthiness principles expands your capacity to receive ever increasing levels of abundance. Allow this to be true and your life will get better.

Help your spouse learn this and both your lives will be expanded even more.

Making sure your kids get exposure to this information will give them better tools to thrive throughout all the ups and downs that life inevitably delivers.

Provide the Worthiness Cycle model to your employees and all of you will be better equipped to absorb the Success that results from good works.

Help your community to realize its worth and you will find that ease and flow will come to you and those around you.

I thought this writing by DavidPaul and Candace Doyle of TheVoiceOfLove.com sums up what has been offered here:

> "You are priceless. The world and everything in it would be incomplete without you. What more value can there be than 'Pricelessness?'
>
> You are irreplaceable and therefore beyond price. Your value is incomprehensible and unchangeable. Since you cannot comprehend it, then you just accept it. Accept it is the Truth and treat yourself as the priceless Everything that you are."
>
> ~ DavidPaul and Candace Doyle

It has been my great pleasure to be your guide on your journey through this book. All the Very Best of Good Fortune to you and your loved ones.

Allan Hunkin
May 2013

P.S. 'Now' is always a good time to get started and if not, in a year from now you may be wishing you had started today.

Bibliography

100 Fascinating Facts You Never Knew About the Human Brain. Nursing Assistant Central.

Carter, D. Neural Networks - the Biological Location of Change. Internet-of-the-Mind.

David R. Hawkins, M. P. (n.d.). Power vs Force: The Hidden Determinants of Human Behaviour.

Dualism. (n.d.).

Robbins, A. *Unleashing The Power Within.*

Additional Resources

The Life Enrichment Series

Your Worthiness Cycle: A Breakthrough Method for Making Consistent Progress Towards Your Goals, Mission and Life Purpose

Other books in the series:

Making Your Worthiness Cycle Work For You In Relationship
Making Your Worthiness Cycle Work For You In Work and Career
Making Your Worthiness Cycle Work For You In Health, Healing and Wellness
The Worthiness Cycle for Teams, Groups and Organizations
Raising Worthy Kids
Your Worthiness And Weight Loss
Finding Better Solutions Faster

Visit Worthiness.com *to learn more*

Teaching The Worthiness Cycle to People We Care About

The first thing that many people do when they finish reading 'Your Worthiness Cycle' is they get excited and want to share this new personal empowerment technology with those that they care about.

It is easy to see that if we take even a little from this book our life will get better in several ways.

People have commented that the book changed everything for them and that they are leading a more abundant life with their spouse, work mates, family and kids a result of reading it.

But I have also found that readers get frustrated because what seems so clear to them is difficult to explain in a way that has as much impact as reading the whole book and spending some mind time on it.

I certainly understand. It took me a long time to come up with the words and visuals to explain this simple but unique and comprehensive understanding of what Worthiness is and how it works. Additionally, many people don't want to take the time to read the book. Many don't learn as well by reading as they do with audio and video teaching aids.

Your Worthiness Cycle 'DVD' is a 55 minute video that teaches the Worthiness Cycle model step by step.

Presented by the author the DVD covers each section of the book plus how the Worthiness Cycle applies to Relationship, Parenting, Health, Wellness as well as Work, Career, Organization and Teams. In less than an hour you can present the benefits of knowing the Worthiness Cycle to your spouse, coffee club and kids. It is perfect for team leaders who want their team to expand their performance and effectiveness.

Your Situation is Unique

Are you stuck? Do you know what to do next? What has 'not' been working about the way you've been attempting to transform situations and challenges in your life that are holding you back? Has reading this book given you new insight that you need further assistance with your situation?

In the past few months I have taken all my research and writings on Worthiness and developed a process combining three personal interviews with reference materials that teach the Worthiness Quotient Model.

I designed the process specifically so as to not create the need for more than three sessions. Everything you need to deal with underlying issues and increase Love, Happiness, Success and Fulfillment and move forward into a new level of abundance is contained within this Three-Step Process.

I want to work with you personally.

First we have an initial interview, (on Skype or landline), where I explain the process in detail, as well as ask a series of questions specific to your situation. As a result we see where your worthiness choke points are, both real ones and imaginary. I'll give you some techniques for you to have an immediate effect on your particular challenges. Sometimes this is all a person needs to transform their situation so that it can progress.

Three Step Counseling / Coaching Sources

Then if you feel you will benefit from a deeper investigation we go *through a Three-Step process* where I do two more interviews and provide you with additional materials you will use to learn the key worthiness principle and assist you in determining the best ways to transform your unique situation into positives in your life.

To lock everything in place we have a follow-up call approximately three weeks later to review and make adjustments unique to your situation.

For some people this three-step process has been nothing short of transformational. The interviews/coaching sessions are 45 minutes in length. With your permission I record each session so you can review later and gain even more awareness and insights over the days, months and years following.

How to Get Started?

Email me at WorthinessNow@gmail.com and I'll reply immediately with more information and pre-interview checklist, (things you will need to have thought a bit about), so our time together will provide you with the best possible outcome.

I look forward to going through this process with you. I know you will gain insights and answers that will have a positive impact on all areas of your life immediately and for years to come.

About Allan Hunkin

Allan is a speaker, writer, broadcaster, coach and consultant in the area of Life Enrichment. He has over thirty years of experience in self help and personal growth. His toolkit for transforming challenges is both wide and deep. He holds credentials and train the trainer status, in five different personal empowerment models.

Allan has been an online broadcaster since 1997 having conducted over 750 interviews with authors and thought leaders in the areas of personal and social transformation and empowerment.

He is the author of three books: 'Where Do I Go From Here?', *'Finding Better Solutions Faster*' and *'Your Worthiness Cycle.'*

Allan lives in Vancouver Canada.

For more information visit: AllanHunkin.com

Facebook	Facebook.com/WorthinessNow
Twitter	Twitter.com/WorthinessNow
YouTube	YouTube/user/allanhunkin
LinkedIn	Linkedin.com/in/allanhunkin

Listen to *'Creating Elegant Solutions'* with Allan Hunkin at: http://www.spreaker.com/user/allanhunkin

www.ingramcontent.com/pod-product-compliance
Lightning Source LLC
Chambersburg PA
CBHW060517030426
42337CB00015B/1920